PROFESSIONAL NEWS WRITING
STUDENT WORKBOOK

COMMUNICATION TEXTBOOK SERIES
Jennings Bryant—Editor

Journalism
Maxwell McCombs—Advisor

PROFESSIONAL NEWS WRITING STUDENT WORKBOOK

Bruce Garrison
Tsitsi Wakhisi
University of Miami

LAWRENCE ERLBAUM ASSOCIATES, PUBLISHERS
1990   Hillsdale, New Jersey   Hove and London

Lawrence Erlbaum Associates, Inc., Publishers
365 Broadway
Hillsdale, New Jersey 07642

ISBN 0-8058-0970-8

Printed in the United States of America
10 9 8 7 6 5 4 3 2 1

Contents

v

Preface

Students and teachers will find a wide range of learning opportunities in this workbook. This book, designed to be the companion assignment book for *Professional News Writing,* also published by Lawrence Erlbaum Associates, Inc., Publishers, contains assignments designed for three different environments.

First, you will find a number of assignments best suited for on-deadline laboratory settings. We feel students should receive a balance of deadline and nondeadline assignments for best development as news writers. These in-class deadline assignments are meant to be completed within a 1- to 2-hour framework.

Second, a number of the assignments has been created with nondeadline, or out-of-laboratory, work in mind. These are best completed when a student has the chance to work at a less harried pace. Some require the full resources of a library, for instance, and are best done out of class.

Third, a small number of assignments requires group involvement. Teamwork in journalism is also an important skill that should be nurtured from the beginning of your journalism education.

How these assignments are utilized will be left to instructors. We feel instructors must serve this course much like an editor or producer who is assigned to work with beginning news writers. Students working independently, however, will easily see which assignments lend themselves to each of these conditions. We have chosen not to label them, however, because of the variety of individual approaches teachers bring to their classes.

The assignments here are based on real-world situations as much as practically possible. We feel some workbooks fail students by using too many artificial situations. We hope this workbook has strength in its real-world news writing foundation.

You will find a number of stories and examples taken from the collegiate press from across the United States. Some of these stories were chosen for their excellence. Some were used because, being written by novices, certain mistakes were made from which we can learn lessons. We have chosen to use *all* college press articles without the writers' names as a result.

We welcome suggestions and comments on this workbook. You may have ideas for improving assignments here. Please feel free to contact us. We may be reached at this address:

School of Communication
University of Miami
P.O. Box 248127
Coral Gables, FL 33124–2030
305–284–2265 (voice)
305–284–3648 (fax)

We certainly encourage your telephone calls and faxes. We invite letters or telephone calls from students. We want your comments, and we hope to be available to you as your consultants as needed.

ACKNOWLEDGMENTS

To write a workbook such as this one, the assistance of many people is required. Thus, there are dozens of professionals who are owed gratitude for their interest and generous gifts of time leading toward production of this work. Our sincerest thanks go out to them and to our students, who have always been willing to lend a hand. For their help in creation of this student workbook, our special thanks to:

Dean Edward Pfister for his assistance in providing the support of the School of Communication at the University of Miami.

Faculty colleague Alan Prince, journalism and media writing professor at the University of Miami, for his timely suggestions.

Robin Weisberg, production editor, Lawrence Erlbaum Associates, for her high quality suggestions for this workbook and the companion textbook.

Randy Stano, director of news-editorial art for *The Miami Herald,* for designing the cover to the books in this set.

Steve Rice, assistant managing editor/graphics, *The Miami Herald,* for providing the *Herald* staff photographs used on the covers of the books.

The Miami Herald and Knight-Ridder, Inc., for permitting access to its computerized library data base, "Vu-Text."

Sherrie Lisitski, graduate student in communication studies at the University of Miami, for her editorial assistance.

Joanne C. Acosta, broadcast journalism student at the University of Miami, for her editorial assistance.

Our families, for their support during the time we needed to complete this workbook.

Bruce Garrison
Tsitsi Wakhisi

Copy Preparation Formats

Newspapers and Magazines

It is important to remember that you may be required to prepare copy without the benefits of computer formatting. Here's the way newspaper and magazine copy is prepared on personal computers and typewriters for news writing classes:

Slug of story
Date submitted
Name of reporter

[This space is left for typesetting instructions]

Uniform copy preparation is essential for the print journalist because of the great quantity of material that is processed by many hands for a single issue of a newspaper or magazine, newsletter, or for a news service report.

In preparing print media stories for this course, this is the format you should follow. Although you will find variations, this is the form generally used for organizations using manual typewriters or personal computers for story composition.

The slug, in the upper left corner, is a short identifying line for your story—something to help headline writers, editors, typesetters, and other story handlers to keep track of the story.

A story about an airplane crash might be tagged "plane" or "crash" or something similar.

(MORE)

1

Slug
Name
Add 1/Page Number (2)

    Avoid slug words that could be applied to several stories, like "city" on a city commission story, or words that would be embarrassing if they somehow got into print.

    The story begins one third of the way down the first page. This gives an editor space to instruct typesetters and other copy handlers on how to treat the story. In your case, it provides room for your instructor's comments and questions.

    Head the second page with the slug, following it with an "Add 1" to indicate it is the first added page (remember, it is really page 2). "Add 2" indicates the second added page (and third page overall).

    Your name should also go on every added page.

    Use a 60-space line, indenting five spaces for paragraphs. You can "program" your word processor to do this by using the margin settings command. This helps you estimate story length in column inches and in time.

    Copy should be double spaced; in fact, some editors-teachers prefer triple spacing. This allows room for editing notations and corrections. Your word processor will also do this automatically for you if you set it properly.

(MORE)

Slug
Name
Add 2/Page Number (3)

Assignments should be written on newsprint (often called copy paper), typing paper, or plain computer paper if you prefer. If you use "track" fanfold paper, remove the tracks and separate the pages.

Do not break a paragraph in going from one page to the next. If you begin a paragraph on one page, finish it on that page. This may be hard to avoid if you are using a word processor. Check the program's default settings.

Always indicate with the word "MORE" that at least one more page follows.

Because it is ambiguous for typesetters, do not end a line with a hyphenated word or a broken hyphenated word series. You can program your word processor to do this, also.

Letter-perfect typing is not required. Editors regard retyping as a waste of time if an error can be corrected by the editing conventions (symbols) that are shown in Appendix F of the textbook.

(MORE)

Slug
Name
Add 3/Page Number (4)

When using a typewriter, do not correct an error by typing over it or erasing it. Strike-overs are ambiguous, and erasing is too time-consuming. Instead, type through the error with a string of "xxxxx's" and go on from there. If you don't spot an error until the line has been typed, pencil in the correction and cross out the mistake.

Computers with word processors also produce "clean"-looking copy that may have hidden errors. Edit carefully!

This should not be taken as an excuse for sloppy work. Clean copy always produces clean typesetting—at least cleaner than a line full of corrections. Above all, make sure your corrections are understandable for the editor and typesetter.

When you come to the end, quit. The graphic symbols "###" or "–30-" tell the editor that there is no more.

########

Radio News Scripts

Here's the way news writing students should prepare radio news scripts in news writing classes:

Story Slug
Writer's name
Date of story
Newscast to be aired
Page number (1)

SCRIPT LENGTH (0:00)

Start your radio script with the story's one-word slug, your name, the date, the edition of the newscast for which the script is prepared (usually indicated by the hour of the day), and the script page number.

Radio news copy should be triple spaced whenever possible. Furthermore, it should be written with liberal spacing on each page of the script. You should never split a sentence or a paragraph over two pages.

At the end of each page, type "(MORE)" or "-END-".

You should place the length of this script on the top of the first page.

(MORE)

Story Slug
Writer's name
Date of story
Newscast to be aired
Page number (2)

When you include an actuality in your story, you should indicate cues like this for the announcer:

ACTUALITY: (PLACE THE ACTUAL WORDS OF THE SPEAKER ON THE TAPE IN CAPS WITHIN PARENTHESES FOR THE ANNOUNCER IN CASE THE CARTRIDGE MACHINE OR CARTRIDGE FAILS TO WORK. SOME STATIONS PREFER IN-CUES AND OUT-CUES ONLY. BE SURE TO INCLUDE THE ACTUALITY'S LENGTH. LENGTH: 0:00).

Because you are typing content to be read over the air in upper and lower case letters, any material, such as directions to the announcer, should be in uppercase.

Direct quotations that are not actualities must have cues for the audience. Phrases such as "quoting Smith" help listeners.

(MORE)

Story Slug
Writer's name
Date of story
Newscast to be aired
Page number (3)

Remember to put any hard-to-pronounce words in phonetic (fo-NET-ik) form for the announcer. Mispronunciations are embarrassing.

Capitalize when in doubt. This also helps reduce inflection problems when someone is reading your script cold—without rehearsal.

On longer scripts and audio packages, don't forget your news department's standard signoff: This is Ann Smith reporting, WVUM-FM News, Coral Gables.

-END-

Television News Scripts

Here's a basic copy format for preparing a television news script used in news writing classes:

Story Slug
Writer's name
Date of story
Newscast to be aired
Page number (1)

THIS SCRIPT'S LENGTH (0:00)

VIDEO	AUDIO
Classroom with some students typing	Start your news script with the story's one-word slug, your name, the date, the edition of the newscast for which the script has been prepared (usually indicated by the hour of the day), and the page number.
Personal computer terminal screen tight shot	Television news copy should be triple spaced whenever possible.

(MORE)

Story Slug
Writer's name
Date of story
Newscast to be aired
Page number (2)

VIDEO	AUDIO
University of Miami journalism prof	(SOT: It is a good idea to use sound on tape—called an S-O-T.)
Tight shot of script page	Furthermore, copy should be written with liberal spacing on each page of the script. You should never split a sentence or a paragraph over two pages.
Close-up shot of student editing a page of copy	At the end of each page, type "(MORE)" or "-END-". You should place the length of this script on the top of the first page.
	(MORE)

Story Slug
Writer's name
Date of story
Newscast to be aired
Page number (3)

VIDEO	AUDIO
File tape of on-air mistake	Remember to put any hard-to-pronounce words in phonetic (fo-NET-ik) form for the announcer. Mispronunciations are embarrassing.
Still file photos of campus TV studio	Capitalize when in doubt. This also helps reduce inflection problems when reading cold—without rehearsal.
	(MORE)

Story Slug
Writer's name
Date of story
Newscast to be aired
Page number (4)

VIDEO	AUDIO
Students editing videotape at editing station	When you include a soundbite in your story, you should indicate cues for the announcer. Type the sound-bite content in parentheses.
Reporter standup close on location in news lab	And on longer scripts and audio packages, don't forget your news department's standard signoff: This is Ted Smith, Channel 51 News, Coral Gables.

INTRODUCTION

1 Working in the News Media

ASSIGNMENT 1.1

Go to your campus or local library. Browse through the current periodical section. Find two magazines: one whose first publication is no older than three years and another that was on the market at least 10 years ago. Write a two-page essay detailing the subject matter and what demand they meet in today's society. Discuss whether they will still be on the market a decade from now.

ASSIGNMENT 1.2

Create a concept for your own new magazine. What would be the subject matter? Where would it circulate? Will it be weekly, monthly, quarterly? Who would be your target audience? What demand does it meet that is not currently being met?

ASSIGNMENT 1.3

Find a magazine (e.g., *Life, National Geographic*) that has been published over several decades. Obtain a recent copy and one issue that is at least 35 years old.

Compare the two, looking at circulation figures, format, size, number of stories, and content. Pay attention to the use of graphics and photos. What differences exist in story selection? Writing style?

ASSIGNMENT 1.4

Monitor the evening network news. Keep a chart similar to the one below. How many commercials? What kind? How long was each one? Time each news item. and describe it. Determine how much time was devoted to news/commercials. Bring your findings to class.

Your chart should be similar to this:

Item Description	Ad News (check one)	Length (Seconds)

Total news time: _____

Total advertising time: _____

ASSIGNMENT 1.5

Dissect the front page of a daily newspaper. How many stories on page 1? How many with bylines? Which stories were accompanied by photos, graphics, or charts? How many stories were above the fold? How many stories jumped? What else is on the page? Promos, index, briefs? Bring your findings to class.

Your chart should be similar to this:

Story Description	Byline or Source	Graphics	Location	Jump	Other

ASSIGNMENT 1.6

Visit your campus radio station. Determine how much time is devoted to news during the day. What kind of news is aired (campus, local, national, international, a combination)? In what proportions? Be able to discuss whether the radio station meets the needs of the university or college community. Include non-news programming in your discussion. Present your conclusions in a 500-word essay.

ASSIGNMENT 1.7

You are applying for a job at your campus newspaper. Editors there want to know how you would handle a basic story. Here's a set of facts and information. Read them over and write a short story of four or five paragraphs. You have 30 minutes. Because of the deadline, you have access to no other information or sources:

The registrar's office at Purdue University Calumet has announced that spring semester enrollment is at an all-time high, with 7,437 students. This compares with 7,160 students last spring. Last fall there were 7,789 students, the second highest fall enrollment at PUC since 1983, when a record 7,830 students were enrolled.

Quote from Lon Larson, registrar: "PUC has put a lot of emphasis on enrollment." Larson attributes this emphasis to the increase in the number of high school graduates attending college. He said that more people are seeing the importance of a college education today.

He cited other reasons for the hike in spring enrollment, including increased local awareness of the PUC campus. He said many of PUC's 15,000 alumni live in the Calumet region and are spreading the word about what the campus has to offer.

ASSIGNMENT 1.8

Using the latest copy of *Editor & Publisher International Year Book,* find your state, and list all of the newspapers published there. Include newspaper publication (daily, morning, and so forth) and circulation figures, who owns the newspaper, and when it was founded. Write a 500-word essay detailing the status of the newspaper industry in your state.

Which newspaper is the largest? Smallest? Add up the total circulation for Sunday editions and compare to the overall population of the state. Are newspapers having a significant impact on the population?

ASSIGNMENT 1.9

Look for a job in current issues of *Editor & Publisher* or *Broadcasting*. They are weekly publications. How many jobs were in the category you selected? What is the pay scale? In general, what are the requirements for the position you want?

ASSIGNMENT 1.10

Using your personal computer and word processor, you are assigned to write your first news story. This news story should demonstrate your own ideas about what is news and how it should be presented.

Writing in newspaper story copy format, prepare an essay discussing the nature of news. In your essay, use recent examples to make stronger points. Try to answer some or all of these questions:

What is news?

What are the elements of news?

How is news determined?

Who decides what is news?

How does technology affect news?

What is *not* news?

What seems to be the most important element of the news-making process?

ASSIGNMENT 1.11

Arrange to talk to a working journalist in your community. Call a newspaper or television reporter and invite this person to talk about what he or she does. Arrange to visit the newsroom and take a tour while you are there. Ask your host why he or she became a journalist. Ask what he or she likes and dislikes about the job.

ASSIGNMENT 1.12

You will probably need the assistance of your instructor to set up this assignment. Some news organizations encourage students to visit with their staff members. See if this is possible in your community.

Spend part of a day on assignment with a reporter. You will have to arrange this in advance, of course, but start by calling the news department of your favorite newspaper, magazine, radio station, or television station.

ASSIGNMENT 1.13

Visit a nearby library or newsstand and obtain several newspapers published on the same day. Compare and contrast coverage. Are the same story subjects on page 1? Are the headlines the same? The story text? Are they presented in similar fashion? Why?

ASSIGNMENT 1.14

As a group project using several videotape recorders, your class should tape ABC, CBS, CNN, and NBC network newscasts for a single evening.

Then watch the programs together (hint: as you record the programs, edit out commercials to save viewing time), and compare and contrast coverage.

Discuss these questions:

Are lead stories the same?

Are the video portions of the stories similar?

Are sources the same?

Are stories ordered in a similar way? Why?

ASSIGNMENT 1.15

Interview a classmate (someone you don't know). Take only 10 minutes. Ask the basics (name, age, year in school, outside jobs, family, reason for being at this school, interests). Be observant: take notes about anything unusual (his one earring; her multicolored hair). Take as many notes as you can. Listen and jot down good, quotable material. Reverse the process and permit your classmate to interview you.

Submit your notes to your instructor for review and comment.

2 News Values

Write an essay on the nature of news and the importance of good, clear writing in the process of news transmission.

This essay should be about three pages in length, drawing from previous classes, this class, your textbook, and AP and UPI print and broadcast stylebooks.

You should also call a professional journalist to ask some questions pertinent to the essay's focus. Include these opinions in your essay. Try a broadcast journalist, magazine journalist, or photojournalist instead of a newspaper journalist if that angle interests you.

Assignment 2.2

Write a one-paragraph definition of news. Is the definition of news different for newspaper journalists? Magazine journalists? Photojournalists? Radio journalists? Television journalists?

Why or why not?

ASSIGNMENT 2.3

Talk to two or three persons you know who are not interested in journalism. Ask each person to define news.

How does each person's answer vary from what you know about news and journalism?

When considering the orientations of journalists and their audiences, are there fundamental values in conflict? If so, what are they?

ASSIGNMENT 2.4

Take a look at the front page of today's newspaper or the cover of one of this week's news magazines. Or, if you prefer, watch the next local newscast. List the stories on the front page, cover, or in the first segment of the newscast. What makes each one newsworthy? What characteristics of news are most dominant? Which are missing?

ASSIGNMENT 2.5

You may need your instructor's assistance in setting up this assignment.

Call a local news organization manager and ask to attend an upcoming daily news meeting when editors or producers discuss the day's news and how it will be covered.

When you have finished attending the meeting, write a brief summary about the process. Try to answer the following questions:

How does the meeting process appear to work?

Who is in charge?

Who sets the agenda?

Who resolves conflicts?

Are editors and producers playing advocacy roles—that is, are they expected to propose and support their ideas and the work of their division's reporters and photographers?

How are decisions made?

ASSIGNMENT 2.6

Identify the news elements in the following leads. Explain your selections. Remember, there are likely to be more than one or two news elements illustrated.

LEAD A: Student Government President Troy Bell was arrested on six counts of driving with a suspended driver's license on the night of Sept. 17 and spent the night in jail, according to Coral Gables Police records.

Bell said he was arrested in a case of mistaken identity. Bail was set at $3,500, but the judge released him on his own recognizance the next morning. Bell is scheduled to return to court Oct. 16.

LEAD B: Former Senator George McGovern attacked the Bush Administration's stance on the defense budget and said the $307 billion presently allocated to defense should be reduced and redistributed.

"The security threat to the United States is greatly reduced," McGovern said before a crowd of approximately 300 last night in the Marvin Center ballroom at the Program Board sponsored event. He added that the probability of a Soviet invasion is comparable to "an invasion from Mars."

LEAD C: State legislation passed in 1987 that would require new teachers to get a master's degree has generated so much controversy that some state legislators are trying to repeal it before it even takes effect.

The Teacher Improvement Act requires all teachers who apply for a continuing certificate beginning in 1992 to earn a master's degree. Currently only a bachelor's degree is required. After graduating from a teaching program, a person can teach for five years with an initial certificate but then must apply for a continuing certificate.

LEAD D: A semester-long seminar series regarding the balance of power for the 1990s entitled "Eye on the Pacific," began last Monday evening in the Carlisle Rogers Business and Economics Building.

According to Seminar Chairperson Dr. John E. Santosuosso, the purpose of the seminar is to give students and members of the community a better understanding of the history, politics, economics, and impact of the Pacific Rim.

LEAD E: The number of students enrolled at PUC this spring semester has reached an all time high, according to the Registrar's office. Spring 1990 enrollment is 7,437 students. Last spring, 7,160 students were enrolled.

ASSIGNMENT 2.7

You are assigned to write Thanksgiving stories for the week of Thanksgiving for the local newspaper. List five story ideas. Which two ideas would work well for television news? Provide details about your approach to coverage. Include likely sources, photographs, and graphics.

ASSIGNMENT 2.8

The following news story is a hard news story. Read it, and then write a short essay explaining why the story is hard news. Next, change the lead (only the lead) to a soft or feature lead.

NEWSPAPER: *The Miami Hurricane,* University of Miami
DATE: Friday, September 29, 1989
VOL. 67, NO. 9
HEADLINE: Senate passes condom bill
PAGE: 1

The Student Government Senate unanimously passed a bill Wednesday that recommends placing condom vending machines in all of the residential college public bathrooms.

The bill was passed in an effort to raise awareness of Acquired Immune Deficiency Syndrome on campus and to make students realize the real danger the disease represents, said SG Attorney General Max Adams.

However, despite enthusiasm on SG's part, Adams said he does not expect the machines to be in the restrooms any time soon. He expects the administration to oppose the placement of condom vending machines in the dorms.

"It's going to be a tough fight," Adams said during his presentation. "It could be a year-long thing."

The bill will now be sent to Dr. William Butler, vice president for Student Affairs, for approval before any further action is taken.

His office has one month to return to the senate with a decision or ask for an extension.

In addition to the vending machines in the residential colleges, Adams said he hopes to start a University-wide AIDS education program and eventually have condom machines in every public restroom on campus.

Adams said he believes there is a real need to educate students about the threat of AIDS. According to Adams, a recent study of college students said one out of every 300 is a carrier infected with the disease. Adams said many who have the disease are completely unaware of it.

The high number of infected students may be caused by students' ignorance of the problem, Adams said.

Dr. Rick Zimmerman, assistant sociology professor, has been studying sexual behavior among college students. During the meeting, Zimmerman said he believes 75 percent of students are sexually active at least once every three to six months. However, only 25 percent of sexually active college students use condoms on a regular basis, according to Zimmerman. He also said those people who expect college students to practice abstinence are being unrealistic.

During his presentation, Adams showed a videotape of former U.S. Surgeon General C. Everett Koop. In the video, Koop made two suggestions to college-aged students.

The first was that the safest sexual relationship is a faithful, monogamous one; the second, that condoms should be used at all times.

"Condoms are not 100 percent protection, but few things in life are," Koop said.

Two new senators were also ratified at Wednesday's meeting. Howie Hauser, a resident assistant in Pearson Residential College, was named the PRC senator. Josh Kotler was accepted as the new apartment area senator.

During Monday's SG Cabinet meeting, Norm Parsons, director of Campus Sports and Recreation, announced plans for the proposed Wellness Center, which would replace the Lane Recreation Center.

The high-tech, multipurpose fitness center will cost an estimated $12 million, none of which has been raised yet, Parsons said.

ASSIGNMENT 2.9

You're not done with the condom story, yet. Go back to the story in Assignment 2.8. You're a copy editor for the campus newspaper, and you've just been told that an important story is developing, which means the condom story has to be trimmed. You've got to take out five paragraphs from this story (or the equivalent of that). Don't cut only from the bottom.

ASSIGNMENT 2.10

Select a story from the local, state, business, sports, or features page of your daily newspaper in which public officials are quoted. These sources don't have to hold elected office. They may be representatives of organizations or prominent citizens. You may also use a local story from page 1. Controversial stories are good, but you needn't limit yourself to a major scam. Many times, reporters and editors make mistakes on the most general of stories.

Call one source mentioned in the story and ask if the information in the story is factual. Was anything taken out of context? If the source is quoted, are the quotes accurate? Do these officials say the story is fair and balanced?

ASSIGNMENT 2.11

If we are to believe what the experts say about timeliness and ethnocentrism, newspapers should have a good number of "local" stories. Using the A section and the local sections of the newspaper, make a chart enumerating the number of international, national, state, and local (metropolitan and county area) stories for one edition.

Try to construct a chart similar to the ones used in Assignments 1.4 and 1.5 to help you in the analysis.

ASSIGNMENT 2.12

Do some trivia reporting. Go out and get the latest news about campus celebrities. Include student government officers, faculty, administrators, and guest speakers on campus. Get personal. Have no fewer than five items. Write the column in a "People and Places" type of format. (Ahem, don't have too much fun with this.)

II | THE BASICS OF NEWS WRITING

3 Writing Leads

With the information provided below, write a news lead for each item. Take a first-day approach. Remember that a news lead is just one or two paragraphs. Select the elements for the lead carefully. You do not have much space for detail. This story is for the next issue of your campus newspaper.

Story No. 1

Meeting of Women in Communication, Inc. planned.

This is the third meeting in a series of six sessions on career problems for women.

Will take place Friday, February 9.

Source is president of club, Miss Johanna Martin, senior in public relations.

Speaker: Psychologist Donna Anderson. Topic: "Working with Men as your Boss."

Meeting is being held in Room 401, Merrick.

This is the campus chapter.

Attendance is free for members. Non-members may donate $2 to attend. Tax deductible.

Business meeting will be held to discuss regional convention trip in April. Will briefly take place before speaker is introduced.

Contact Martin at 555–3455.

Story No. 2

As you know, tuition is being increased 9.8% next year, the provost announced last month.

Some students are upset. A protest is planned.

A group of students will sit in at the driveway of President Edward T. Foote's home (3774 N. Kendall Drive) in Coral Gables in southeast Dade County.

This will happen beginning at 7 o'clock in the morning, Tuesday, February 6. Not sure when it will end.

"We hope to keep him from leaving his house"—words of group leader Linn Topez. Topez is an architecture major and leader of Tuition Trauma, a new group formed this month on campus.

Topez expects 500 students to be there.

A list of demands will be presented. Live local television news is going to be there, Topez claims.

Foote will be a "hostage" at home until he agrees to keep increase equal to cost of living increase this year.

Story No. 3

Parking lot of Eaton residential college will be closed for three days.

This starts at 6 in the morning Wednesday, February 7.

University says the lot must be repainted and repaved to add five new spaces and an access control gate.

Parking in lot near Metrorail station and apartments area is recommended.

Cars still in lot will be towed at expense of owner.

Information provided by Parking Office of Public Safety Department. Parking Director is Jane Gailey.

ASSIGNMENT 3.2

Pick up today's newspaper and critically analyze the leads on page 1. What kind of lead did each reporter use? Is it appropriate for the story? Is it effective? Does it invite you to read the rest of the story?

ASSIGNMENT 3.3

Listen to a radio newscast. What type of leads are being used on the stories you hear? Do they set up the stories for listeners? Do they try to tell too much?

ASSIGNMENT 3.4

Watching your favorite local newscast, listen to the leads on the major stories of the day. How are they written? What is the focus? Are they long or short? Are they to the point? Can they be improved?

ASSIGNMENT 3.5

Find a recent copy of your campus newspaper. Can you rewrite any of the leads to improve them? Is the focus misplaced on any of the leads? If so, how? What makes them better the second time? Select five leads and rewrite them to be stronger.

ASSIGNMENT 3.6

Select a lead to a news story that has a high level of appeal to you personally. Why do you like it? What makes it better than others in the same newspaper, magazine, or newscast?

ASSIGNMENT 3.7

Change the following passive leads to active voice:

A. UCF Student Body President Fred Schmidt was elected Chairman of State Council of Student Body Presidents for the Florida Student Association.

B. After six weeks of complaining, protests, and a trip to Tallahassee, UF women's rights groups were placated Wednesday when Infirmary Director Boyd Kellett agreed to include a special place for women in his new plans for Student Health Services.

C. The Hippodrome State Theatre has received $37,000 in the first 10 days of a fund-raising effort to keep its doors open, Hippodrome officials said at a news conference Wednesday.

D. The title "Ambassador for Epilepsy" has recently been bestowed upon a UW professor by two international groups devoted to helping people with epilepsy.
Dr. Rene H. Levy, chairman and professor of pharmaceutics for the UW School of Pharmacy, was recognized for his work and research in epilepsy by the International Bureau for Epilepsy and the International League Against Epilepsy. The honorary title acknowledges his "excellent work on behalf of all people with epilepsy," said Dr. F. E. Dreifuss, International League Against Epilepsy president from the University of Virginia School of Medicine.

E. A milestone for the UW Medical Center was achieved yesterday when the first liver transplant in the four-state region of Washington, Alaska, Montana and Idaho was performed.
The surgery was led by Dr. James D. Perkins, associate professor of surgery and director of the Division of Transplantation in the Department of Surgery at the UW School of Medicine.

F. Several key issues were decided at this week's NCAA Convention in Dallas. The much maligned Prop 42 was modified, seasons and practice periods were shortened, and penalties for drug violations were stiffened.
These major changes will affect college athletics in the 1990s.

G. A Daytona white-supremacist skinhead was found guilty Tuesday of beating a Gainesville man in April and was sentenced to 60 days in jail, a year's probation, and 200 hours of community service for the crime.
James V. Cleary, 18, cried as a bailiff led him from the courtroom after being sentenced for the beating of 44-year-old Arthur Davis.

H. FSC students are being asked to help provide one of the most precious gifts of all: the ability to read.
FSC and the Center for Adult Literacy are joining forces to offer tutoring to people in the community who are interested in participating in the program called LOOK—Literacy: Opportunities Of All Kinds.

I. In a surprise move to almost everyone present, impeachment proceedings were initiated against Student Government President Troy Bell by a student petition during Wednesday's SG Senate meeting.

The petition cited seven possible violations of the SG Constitution by Bell as grounds for impeachment, including abuse of his authority, misappropriation of SG funds, conduct unbecoming of a member of SG, and ineligibility to hold SG office due to substandard grades.

J. On Sunday, Feb. 4, one of the biggest names in African-American history was honored for her courage and grace.

Rosa Parks, the mother of the civil rights movement, was honored in a tribute on her 77th birthday by hundreds of well-wishers. The event was moderated by the chair of the Democratic National Committee Black Caucus, Dr. C. Delores Tucker.

ASSIGNMENT 3.8

Identify any of the five Ws and H in the following leads:

A. A number of GW student groups recently expressed frustration about the removal, obstruction or defacement of their flyers announcing upcoming activities.

B. Students who are exposed to live concerts, blasting stereos, booming car radios, or loud headphones may not be able to hear a bird sing by the time they reach age 40.
Experts assembled by the National Institutes of Health said exposure to occupational and recreational noises can cause "irreversible and untreatable hearing damage."

C. Amidst a mob of television reporters, photographers, and well-wishers, Soviet politician Boris Yeltsin entered the banquet room of the Omni International Hotel Sunday and immediately began to work the crowd.

D. A man charged with the attempted murder of a University of Miami police officer will plead not guilty to all charges when he goes to court Monday, his lawyer said. However, according to police reports, the suspect signed a confession.

E. West German students at Memphis State University view the recent developments in the political situation of East Germany and other Warsaw Pact nations with hopes and anticipation.

F. The UW evening degree program scheduled to start this fall may not serve as many students as expected unless the Washington Legislature comes up with more money, according to Richard Lorenzen, vice provost and director of UW Extension.

G. Student Government President Troy Bell was arrested on six counts of driving with a suspended driver's license on the night of Sept. 17 and spent the night in jail, according to Coral Gables Police records.

H. Former Senator George McGovern attacked the Bush Administration's stance on the defense budget and said the $307 billion presently allocated to defense should be reduced and redistributed.

I. State legislation passed in 1987 that would require new teachers to get a master's degree has generated so much controversy that some state legislators are trying to repeal it before it even takes effect.

J. A semester-long seminar series regarding the balance of power for the 1990s entitled, "Eye on the Pacific," began last Monday evening in the Carlisle Rogers Business and Economics Building.

ASSIGNMENT 3.9

Broadcast Leads: Choose any five of the leads in ASSIGNMENT 3.8 taken from student newspapers and change them to leads suitable for broadcast.

ASSIGNMENT 3.10

Spelling Test

The following words are listed in the *Associated Press Stylebook*. Look them up, even if you are certain about the spelling. Correct any mistakes.

Some words should be capitalized, others should not. The same applies for hyphens. Others may be two words instead of one, or vice versa.

1.	cigarette	2.	innocuous
3.	popsicle	4.	t-shirt
5.	zip code	6.	ten-fold
7.	parishioner	8.	harrasment
9.	chaufeur	10.	able-bodied
11.	coup d'etat	12.	innoculate
13.	riffraff	14.	vacuum
15.	year-long	16.	teammate
17.	news stand	18.	good-bye
19.	changeable	20.	acknowledgement
21.	cupfuls	22.	judgement
23.	restaurateur	24.	wartime
25.	wrongdoing	26.	supercede
27.	nighttime	28.	fusellage
29.	carefree	30.	accomodate
31.	cureall	32.	catsup
33.	sacrilegious	34.	washed-up
35.	boo-boo	36.	facade
37.	men's wear	38.	stopgap
39.	workweek	40.	alledge
41.	dependant	42.	knowhow
43.	see-saw	44.	wherever
45.	allright	46.	detente
47.	Laundromat	48.	sargeant
49.	smolder	50.	bonafide
51.	exaggerate	52.	livable
53.	skilfull	54.	besiege
55.	A.M.	56.	donut
57.	diarrhea	58.	limosine
59.	likeable	60.	sherrif
61.	sizable	62.	amidst
63.	dilema	64.	liaison
65.	amuck		

ASSIGNMENT 3.11

Write leads based on the following information.

A. Florida Rep. David Flagg, D-Gainesville, has introduced a bill to the state Legislature that would ban smoking on all state college campuses, including outdoors and in dormitories. If the bill is approved, faculty and student smokers would have to leave campus, which could be as much as a 15-minute walk, before they could have a cigarette. The proposal allows for a two-year grace period, permitting smokers to light up outdoors. But by July 1992, a person would have to leave campus to smoke. Administrators at universities and community colleges said that while the bill has good health implications, such restrictions may be unfair.

B. Woodstock producer John Morris will speak today at 8 p.m. in the Reitz Union's Rion Ballroom. Morris will detail the difficulties involved in producing history's biggest musical event. The presentation will feature a lecture, slides, the movie "Woodstock," and a question and answer session. Morris' talk coincides with the 20th anniversary. In August 1969, more than a half million people invaded Max Yasgur's dairy farm near Bethel, New York. The concert site was about 60 miles from Woodstock. Morris also will discuss backstage stories about rock'n'roll legends Jimi Hendrix, The Grateful Dead, Santana, and The Who.

ASSIGNMENT 3.12

Critique the following leads. Look at them carefully. The problem may not be a missing Who, What, Where, Why, When or How. If you like the lead, defend your position.

A. "Knock, knock. . .Who's there?

"Sherwood . . . Sherwood who?

"Sure would like to win Miss UCF," said Jennifer Okaty during the interview portion of the Miss UCF Scholarship pageant 1990. Hours later, Okaty won the pageant.

B. A fraternity party ended early Saturday morning when an unidentified man fired gunshots into the house, Gainesville police said.

C. "I didn't come here to make you come to your feet," Rev. Tyrone L. Crider told about 100 students Tuesday. "I came here to make you come to your senses."

D. Once again National Condom Week raises its proverbial head. Speakers, workshops, and information tables will be in full force this week illustrating the importance of safe sex to college students.

E. Between 7 and 9 p.m. tonight, a group of concerned students will make an annual survey around campus, taking note of potential problem areas due to inadequate lighting or overgrown shrubbery.

Nightwalk 1990, sponsored by the ASUW Committee on Crime Prevention, is a one-night program designed to locate where potential crimes could occur on campus and to get students involved in making the campus a safer place to walk at night.

ASSIGNMENT 3.13

Here are your notes, including quotations, regarding a tuition hike story you were assigned. Come up with the lead.

Undergraduate and graduate tuition will be increased for the next school year by 9.8%. Tuition, including fees, will be $13,050, up from $11,801 for the current year. Room and board also will go up by 8%.

The announcement was made by University of Miami provost and executive vice president Luis Glaser yesterday. Glaser said the University of Miami Board of Trustees has approved the increase.

UM Student Government President Troy Bell opposed the administration's plans.

"It's disgusting. Tuition is up 9.8 percent. At the same time UM is basking in the popularity of its $400 million (fundraising) campaign."

"A critical mistake was made by the upper echelons of the administration," Bell also said.

The increase is part of a 5-year financial plan in which tuition increases each of the 5 years, with the rate of the increase declining each of those years, said Glaser. However, this approved increase is equal to last year's. The plan originally called for a 9.7% increase for next year.

"The crystal ball is cloudy . . . some things are hard to predict. Much of the calculations are based on unknowns," said Glaser.

4 | Story Organization

Today you are working under deadline. You must get the attached stories written and printed out to submit to your editor by the end of class. Your publication is a small afternoon newspaper. Thus, your stories will be published later today. Keep the date and your readers in mind.

Since your teacher is providing the information here, assume that the city editor is your teacher. Be sure to write quickly but accurately, and leave yourself time to edit and check your work.

Fact List #1

1. Hold up just before 9:00 this morning at Kentucky Fried Chicken, Dixie Highway and North Canal Drive.

2. Occurred when manager was opening up. Manager identified as Carlos Alberto Sanchez, who says he is from Homestead.

3. Young man armed with switch blade did it. Manager was also young, 27. This man got away and is not identified.

4. $456 taken in cash and some checks (the amount in checks is unknown). He also took a bag full of cold chicken.

5. No one was hurt.

6. Information comes from Homestead Police Department public information officer (Robert S. Villar). He is a sergeant.

7. First time this store has been robbed. Been open since 1982.

Fact List #2

1. Burglary at Miami-Dade Community College Homestead campus discovered this morning.

2. Safe in bursar's office was opened in the Frederick L. Ashley Building with an acetylene torch that was left behind.

3. Burglars came through the ceiling tiles.

4. Safe was ruined.

5. Employee in office forgot to turn on the security system for the office at closing yesterday.

6. Cash taken totaled about $11,500 cash, $7,300 checks, and $200 coins.

7. Information comes from Metro-Dade Police Department PIO Dennis Kent.

8. Estimated time and date of theft cannot be determined.

9. Dean Edward Thomas was in the building late last night and says he did not hear anything unusual.

10. Professor Edna Schoenfeld was in her office for a meeting after a night class but says she did not hear anything out of the ordinary either. Custodial staff questioned by police did not detect any unusual activity.

ASSIGNMENT 4.2

For next class, work on this assignment on story organization. The purpose is to study some of the differences in the major news story forms.

Part One

Find a local newspaper and get some scissors and paste. Look through your newspaper for some examples of the story forms discussed in class (listed below). Mount each story on a sheet of paper, then write a paragraph on each one, explaining why you think it is an example of the particular type. Length is not important here. Find:

a. Inverted pyramid.
b. Chronological.
c. Suspended interest.
d. Story involving controversy, displaying an attempt at balance.
e. Essay.

Part Two

Also in that newspaper, clip some stories for the purpose of outlining each in detail to show its structure.

a. Select one that is 1–5 paragraphs in length.
b. Select one that is 6–10 paragraphs in length.
c. Select one that is 10–20 paragraphs in length.

Again, cut and paste the story on copy paper, then write your analysis on each selection. Explain its organizational form, if any, and itemize each paragraph's purpose.

ASSIGNMENT 4.3

Write a story from the following information. You will want to incorporate all five items in whatever way you feel is best. This should challenge your story organization skills.

The information is provided by Dr. William Newmark, supervisor of the Emergency Room at Jackson Memorial Hospital. Activity covers the most recent 24-hour period ending at 8 a.m. today.

Item No. 1: At 1:15 p.m. Alton Hammond, 10, admitted and treated for gunshot wound in the mouth. Mother drove him to hospital. Condition now satisfactory.

Was riding bicycle on the 8000 block of NW 22nd Avenue, near his home (1655 W. Flagler St.), when hit. Rode home and told mother. Never saw who fired, but heard crack of shot. Lost two front teeth and a bit of upper lip. Apparently a small caliber weapon. A little plastic surgery and his lip will be as good as new. His mom was really angry. Weird things go on in their neighborhood, she said. Mother's name is Miriam Henderson.

Item No. 2: At 3:25 p.m., City of Miami Police Officer Brady Burkett, 39, admitted with pinched nerve in his back. Surgery is planned after he spends about 24 hours in traction. He stopped Calvin Elsabroke on Dallas Street near Biscayne Boulevard for supposedly running through a stop sign.

Officer bent down at side of Elsabroke's car after asking for license and the pain hit him. Doubled over and couldn't straighten up.

Asked Elsabroke to go down to squad car and radio for ambulance, which he did. Attendants found him kneeling in pain in street, with Elsabroke directing traffic around him.

They relaxed him a bit with a shot and brought him to ER pretty well sedated. No, he didn't give Elsabroke a ticket.

Item No. 3: At 8:48 p.m., Metro-Dade Patrolman Antonio Laughton brought in Ricky Harcle, 7, of 3570 SW 9th Terr., in squad car. Child was DOA. Was riding on back of dad on motorcycle on Palmetto Expressway at SW 24th Street and fell off.

The boy's father, Andrew Harcle, went about a quarter mile before he could stop. Ran back to get Ricky, but it was too late. Several cars had run over him but none stopped.

Laughton happened by right after Harcle picked the boy up and drove them here. Boy was alive at scene. Coroner John S. Starnes is now involved. He'll have to determine the cause of death.

Item No. 4: At 9:20 p.m., Brad Weirstir, 16, was brought in by Silver Streak Ambulance Service. He's bad off. Still listed as extremely critical. Had immediate brain surgery.

Was in woodworking class at Edison High School. A block of wood he was working flew out of a lathe and smacked him above the left ear. Collapsed and has never regained consciousness. Paramedics stabilized him on the scene.

Dr. Ed Stromfur, who's on the case, recommends another operation this afternoon if the lad's condition doesn't improve by then.

Item No. 5: At 10:05 p.m., Sharon Brackett, 31, of 626 Grand Concourse in Miami Shores, admitted after a freak accident in her own garage. Her car wouldn't start when she headed to the Farm Store. Raised hood to short the starter solenoid by jumping current through a screwdriver. Had left car in gear. It shot forward, pinning her against the garage wall.

The engine was running, and she was held jammed there for about two hours until a next-door neighbor, Andres Martinez, heard her yelling. Suffered a fractured left thigh, smashed right knee cap, two cracked ribs, and multiple contusions on body. Her doctor, Thomas Winton, lists her condition as stable.

ASSIGNMENT 4.4

Clip several news stories from your local or campus newspaper. After attaching them to a sheet of paper, outline the major sections of the articles. How are they organized? Do you see how the author assembled the parts of the story? What are the strengths and weaknesses of each story's organizational approach?

ASSIGNMENT 4.5

Locate a newspaper or magazine news story that you feel is poorly organized. Clip the story out, a paragraph at a time, and reorganize it.

How has it improved? What were the flaws in the original organizational plan?

ASSIGNMENT 4.6

Find examples of news stories that each represent inverted pyramid, chronological, or essay organizational approaches. Are the organizational approaches appropriate for the stories you have selected?

ASSIGNMENT 4.7

Identify news stories that combine the basic organizational approaches. Can you find any stories that use Roy Peter Clark's "hourglass" approach to organizing information?

ASSIGNMENT 4.8

Organization is aided by transitions. Find a news story that does not use transitions in an effective way or, perhaps, does not use them at all. Rewrite and reorganize the information in that story using transitions.

ASSIGNMENT 4.9

Rewrite the following sentences, employing Time-Date-Place sequence:

1. The University of Miami Innovation and Entrepreneurship Institute will present a Business Forum on Thursday, April 26 (2 weeks from now) at 6 p.m. at the Hyatt Regency Hotel, 400 S.E. Second Ave., featuring First Pass Diagnostic Inc. Cost of the dinner is $15.

2. The Dade school system's Child Guidance, Care and Management Services Advisory Committee will hold its meeting in Conference Room 807 of the School Board Administration Building, 1450 N.E. Second Ave., at 9:30 a.m. Wednesday.

3. The Dade County School Board will hold its next regular meeting on Feb. 7 at 1 p.m. in the first-floor auditorium of the School Board Administration Building, 1450 N.E. Second Ave.

4. The University Behavioral Center will offer a community seminar on common eating disorders tonight from 7 p.m. to 9 p.m. at the center.

5. The Central Florida World of Clowns Inc. will offer an eight-week course called "The Art of Clowning 101." The class will be held once a week every Tuesday evening from 7 p.m. until 9 p.m. at the Student Center, Room H.

ASSIGNMENT 4.10

Here is the information on which you may base a set of news briefs. Remember to follow the Time-Date-Place sequence in your stories. (Don't make up information, quotations, or sources.)

Item 1: The Society of the Sigma Xi annual banquet will be on Thursday (this week) at 7 p.m. at the Commons of the University of Miami's Rosenstiel School of Marine and Atmospheric Science, 4600 Rickenbacker Causeway. The Sigma Xi Professor of the Year will be named.

Item 2: The Tribal Arts Society announces a lecture on "Sacred Promises: The Meaning of Mexican Masks" at the University of Miami's Lowe Art Museum, 1301 Stanford Drive. The speaker will be Janet Esser, professor of art history at San Diego State University. The lecture begins at 8 p.m. Wednesday, April 11. The lecture is free for members of the society. Admission is $5 for non-members and guests.

Item 3: The Young Lawyers Section of the Dade County Bar Association will present three talks at the University of Miami Law School. The National Law Week presentations are open to all law students as well as undergraduate students and members of the general public. They will be held in Room 109 at 12:30 p.m. each day. The presentations:

April 17: Janet Reno, state attorney for Dade County, and Bennett Brummer, the public defender for Dade County. The two will speak on Law Week's theme: "Generations of Justice."

April 19: Three in-house corporate attorneys will speak on the legal and practical requirements for obtaining a position in the corporate world in general and at their respective companies. Speakers include Nancy Henry of Florida Power & Light Co.; Dorian Denburg of Southern Bell, and Paul Dee, general counsel of the University of Miami.

April 20: Speakers will discuss the legal and practical requirements for obtaining a position with real estate development companies. Speakers include Rob Kaplan from Terra Nova, Morris Watsky from Lennar, and Ted Brown from Arvida.

Item 4: Two workshops sponsored by the Center for Instructional and Research Computing Activities will take place next week from 1:55 to 2:45 p.m. in Room 337 of the Reitz Student Union. The workshops are designed to help graduate students who want to type their own thesis or dissertation on a microcomputer. The workshops will provide information on using sample thesis files and handouts. No registration is necessary. Next Tuesday (use next Tuesday's date) the session will be for students interested in producing a thesis using Macintosh's Microsoft Word. Next Thursday's session is for those thesis writers interested in using WordPerfect on a PC.

Item 5: The Coral Gables Chamber of Commerce trustees council invites the public to attend its meeting Friday (this week) at the Danielson Gallery of the Biltmore Hotel at 7:45 a.m. Florida Commissioner of Education Betty Castor will speak. Admission is $20 per person.

Item 6: Students may get assistance in preparing their income tax returns from the Volunteer Income Tax Association, which is offering the services of certified public accountants and accounting students from the University of Miami. The service is provided every day from 9 a.m. to 3 p.m. through April 16 at the Student Union, Room 240.

Item 7: Internships are available in business and banking, legal work, politics, social work, education, health care, psychiatry, communication, and the fashion industry through a Summer Internship in London program. A meeting to discuss this opportunity will be held at Pearson Residential College March 6 at 8 p.m. The meeting is being organized by the Office of International Programs and will be hosted by Ian Watkins, director of the University of Miami Summer Internships in London.

Item 8: A series of workshops sponsored by college feminists in South Florida will be held March 23–25 at the Dupont Plaza Hotel, 300 Biscayne Blvd. Way. Sessions will run from 9 a.m. to 4 p.m. daily. Dr. Janet M. Canterbury, nationally known leader in the feminist movement and deputy dean for medical education at the University of Miami's School of Medicine, will be the main speaker.

Participants may register at the conference site or at any of the following institutions: The University of Miami, Miami-Dade Community College, or Florida International University. Preregistration fee is $10. On-site registration is $15 for students with a valid identification card. Cost to the general public is $25. The following topics will be discussed during the workshop: Abortion for Survival, Date/Acquaintance Rape, Sexism in Language, and Men in Feminism.

Item 9: The Hillel Jewish Center is sponsoring a musical Oneg Shabbat at Pearson Residential College at 6:30 p.m. today. Tomorrow (use today and the day of the week for tomorrow) night there will be a Latin Jewish Extravaganza. All students 12–25 are invited to indulge in food and music. The event will begin at 9 p.m. in the center, 1100 Stanford Drive. Admission will be $15.

Item 10: The French Club of the University of Miami will host a meeting at 6 p.m. March 29 in Memorial Classroom Building, Room 205. Jean C. Michel, a Ph.D. from the State University of New York and a specialist in Caribbean Studies, will present a lecture in French on the history of Haiti and will give an explanation of the play, "La Tragedie du Roi Christophe." Michel will also appear at 7 p.m. April 6–7 at the Miami-Dade Community College, 300 N.E. 2nd Ave.

ASSIGNMENT 4.11

The paragraphs in the following stories are not in the order they were in when the story was published. Organize them into what you consider the best presentation of information and quotes.

Item 1: From *The Daily* of the University of Washington.

Senate Bill 6553, sponsored by Senate Higher Education Committee Chairman Jerry Saling, R-Spokane, would redirect responsibility of branch campus upper-division program and baccalaureate degrees to the regional universities and the state colleges.

In last year's session, UW and WSU were given administrative control over these programs. However, Saling believes that the regional and state colleges have the potential to administer these degrees at a lower cost.

The bill would redesignate the UW's and WSU's role in branch campus education by directing them to provide graduate level programs and degrees for the branch campuses.

UW administrators could face a tough battle against a bill which would rewrite branch campus history by taking administrative control from the UW and Washington State University and placing it in the hands of the regional universities and state colleges.

"I will do everything that I can to see that that is not done, and so if that means different organizations running branch campuses, well, then I'll fight for that," Saling said.

At a public hearing held Wednesday in Olympia, Saling explained the reasoning behind his bill to Bob Edie, UW director of Government Relations.

Saling fears the Legislature will not be able to meet branch campus needs without cutting back on other areas of higher education.

Edie reminded Saling that a substantial majority of both the House and the Senate voted last year to give UW and WSU those responsibilities.

The bill would also require that the degrees not indicate at which campus the degree was granted.

"We believe the state should now move into implementing those responsibilities, and we would hope we were past the discussion," Edie said.

Item 2: From *The Hilltop,* Howard University.

The audience's response to *Do the Right Thing* was extremely positive. The audience viewer, Jan Tax, stated, "I have seen all of Lee's movies, but this is by far the best."

"A thought-provoking movie," said Roberta Martin, another viewer.

On Feb. 1 and 2, the AFI featured Lee's first major work, *Joe's Bedstuy Barbershop: We Cut Heads*. That film was his graduate thesis while at New York University.

In honor of Black History Month, the American Film Institute Theatre, located in the Kennedy Center's Hall of States, presented a special tribute to filmmaker Spike Lee.

Robyn Leary, publicist for the AFI, said that her organization chose Lee because "he is a prominent filmmaker of the decade."

"His work is brave and original; we salute his bravery in filmmaking," Leary said.

By featuring Lee's movies, the AFI hopes to expose all people to his work. "Sometimes people have the idea that the American Film Institute Theatre is exclusive. Lee's work helps us to reach all people in different communities," she said.

Leary added that Lee is supposedly going to visit the theater in the next two weeks, but they are waiting to hear from him.

Dr. Lawrence Clunie, a Howard graduate and dentist, said, "I had mixed emotions about the movie; I felt sorry for the Italian owner because he knew the kids in the neighborhood.

"However, the Italian owner could not understand the need for him to represent their culture in his restaurant," he said.

"Because he could not identify with their culture, he was surprised by the extreme measures that black youth took to make their point," Clunie added.

"Do the Right Thing," released last summer, was the first to be presented last week. As the temperature rose in the movie, so did the racial, economic and cultural tensions in the Bedford Stuyvesant neighborhood of Brooklyn.

The AFI, which is celebrating its 25th year, was established to celebrate the moving image as an art form, Leary said. The AFI features 750 movies a year. There is a show every night of the week.

On Feb. 22 at 6:30 p.m. and Feb. 24 at 3 p.m., the AFI will show its last presentation of Lee's *School Daze*. Tickets are $6.

Item 3: From *The Central Florida Future,* University of Central Florida, Orlando (College Press Service).

Amherst President Peter Pouncey and UMass Chancellor Joseph Duffey, for instance, issued a joint statement blasting an annual snowball fight between Amherst and UMass students at the first snowfall of each winter. At that time, UMass students marched three miles to the Amherst campus to engage in battle.

Administrators hope a show of force by local police, who have promised to put additional officers on duty the night of the first big snow, will dampen the warriors' ardor.

"This is not a venerable tradition," Amherst spokeswoman Terry Allen explained. "It's a criminal event."

Hoping to avoid a repeat of mass student snowball fights that turned violent and destructive at a number of campuses, administrators at Amherst College and the universities of Idaho and Massachusetts-Amherst are pleading with students to keep their hands out of the snow.

"We have asked police for help," reported spokesman Terry Maurer of the University of Idaho, where last winter's first snowfall turned into a violent three-day clash between dorm residents and greeks.

"The administration doesn't want it to happen (again), and a lot of students don't want it to happen," he noted.

Idaho's annual snowball fight last year deteriorated into a "three-day riot," said Ray Horton, president of the Residence Hall Association. Damages, mostly in the form of broken windows, amounted to nearly $5,000.

The Amherst fight caused nearly $2,000 in damages to Amherst College buildings.

"Something went wrong the first night," Horton recounted, "and the next two nights were spent trying to get people back for what happened the first night." In addition to tossing snowballs, Horton added, students were tossing firecrackers and rocks.

An Amherst student, Gary Gonya, was nearly blinded in one eye. He has since become a crusader of sorts, writing open letters to students at both schools in hopes of discouraging another exchange.

Gonya said he was most likely hit by a snow-packed rock. A year after the injury, his vision in the damaged eye is only 50 percent of normal.

"We need to either change the tone of the fight or get rid of it," Gonya said.

Both snowball battles started out as little more than an excuse to play outside in the snow.

"The fights are inherently fun," Gonya said, "but it's become somewhat deranged in the animosity and destructiveness."

Students apparently took the plea to heart. There have been no large-scale snow battles on the campus since then.

Official pleadings can help. A snowball fight that injured several students and caused property damage at the University of Nebraska in early 1988 prompted NU administrators to send letters to students last November asking them not to engage in a mass snowball fight.

ASSIGNMENT 4.12

Explain how the following story from *The Daily Helmsman,* Memphis State University, illustrates the essay approach to news story organization. Is the ending a wrap up that summarizes and makes the case one last time?

NEWSPAPER: *The Daily Helmsman,* Memphis State University
DATE: Wednesday, October 18, 1989
VOL.: 53, No.: 36
HEADLINE: Researchers study problems faced by interracial couples
PAGE: 1

Dating can be a confusing experience for anyone, but couples of different races encounter problems unlike those found in traditional relationships.

People involved in interracial relationships say companionship is what they find in a mate, but researchers have other theories as to why people find mates from other races.

Michael McCray, 22, a freshman in mechanical engineering, dated a white woman for three years, but he said they were friends first. They had classes and studied together.

"She wasn't into interracial things. I brought it up by joking with one of her friends, and she seemed interested in me. She is from Tennessee and her parents don't believe in interracial relationships. So, her parents didn't know, but mine did, and she came to my house lots of times," McCray said.

Since he attended a predominantly white high school, McCray said he dated white girls in the band, since "It's basically who you hang out with."

McCray talked about how people react when they see an interracial couple but do not know the people involved.

"Black females look at you funny when you're together and some of my partners got in my face in the beginning," he said.

"A lot of people believe (it should be) blacks with blacks and whites with whites. I don't look for white girls, but it's hard to talk to black girls. It's hard dealing with the public. I think we're all a little prejudiced to some degree," McCray said.

Darryl Tukufu, professor of sociology at Memphis State University, said available data shows that interracial marriages involve people of the same social status. He said it is a myth that the couple is marrying up or marrying down when choosing a person of a different ethnic background.

"Some African-American men do it for ego-status attainment. There is also the desirability of Nordic features and the forbidden fruit—the Euro-American woman that has been forbidden for so long," he said.

Lisa Dodson, 20, a sophomore in education, is currently involved with a black man. She said her last relationship with a black man lasted three years and was based on friendship, not novelty.

Dodson said the first black man she dated she had known since kindergarten.

"After being with someone for a long time it stops being cute or different. In fact, you lose sight of being different until people remind you of it."

In 1987, 72 percent of interracial marriages were between black males and white females. Tukufu said an increase is possible with more social interaction, but in the South most people marry within their own group.

"I did a study at Northeastern University that showed the more African-Americans, especially males, that go outside their race, the less consciousness they have. As the social interaction increases, their social awareness and cultural pride decreases," Tukufu said.

He said studies show fear of social disapproval keeps the trend down for white men dating black women.

Stephen Griego, 21, a senior in English, said, "The next time I do date someone out of my race, it is going to have to be someone I really care about, otherwise it's not worth it. White people who don't like it try to ignore you. Black people who don't like it let you know."

"That goes bad both ways because white girls think you are only interested in black girls, and black girls think you are trying to make them part of an experiment," he said. Dodson said she dated within her own race as well and has no qualms about telling the white men she dates about the other men.

"I tell a white guy that I do date black guys because I want them to know, and I want to see how they react because they may not be someone I want to go out with," she said.

Eric Sawyer, 22, a junior in political science, studied the ethnic consumer market for two years. His study was based on interaction between the racial groups. "To get to the heart, we had to understand how they related to each other," Sawyer said.

He proposed a theory comparing the historic field slave to black people who live in predominantly black areas such as Whitehaven. Black people living in Germantown are compared to "house slaves" who assimilated with whites more often and were separated from other "slaves." Sawyer said some members of one group are more comfortable with ones from the other.

Sawyer contributed economics and education to the mix also.

"Most black women in college see themselves as aspiring higher than the black man," he said.

In a 1983 study at Morris-Brown College in Atlanta, the behavioral patterns of white females and black males proved more compatible, and answers given by black females were more similar to answers given by white males.

"As these people became more in control of economic situations due to income and college experience, rates of progress are similar and there is more interaction between the two groups," Sawyer said.

Reprinted with the permission of *The Daily Helmsman*, Memphis State University.

ASSIGNMENT 4.13

Use bullets to highlight the major issues in Proposition 42's impact on college athletics. You will be provided enough information from a story published in *The Daily Helmsman,* Memphis State University, to write the entire story.

College athletics in the 1990s will be affected by a number of major changes in Proposition 42. The key controversial issues decided at this week's NCAA Convention in Dallas will require sessions and practice periods to be shortened, and tougher penalties for drug violations. Two major issues that were not approved centered on eligibility. One called for allowing Proposition 48 "victims" a fourth year of eligibility if these players had accumulated 105 semester hours of credit by the end of four years.

The measure failed for the most part because delegates said it totally defeated the purpose of the rule. The other failed issue concerned taking eligibility away from freshmen in Division I basketball so that these athletes could have ample time to adjust to the academic rigors of college before having to devote their time to basketball.

Proposition 42 before the amendment required incoming freshman athletes to have a C average in core high school courses and minimum ACT or SAT scores to be given athletic scholarships.

Now, partial qualifiers, or those who passed one of the requirements but not both, will be eligible for regular school financial aid but not athletic scholarships. Before they were ineligible for both.

Beginning in August 1992, basketball teams will be allowed to start practice on Nov. 1 (previously Oct. 15). They will not be allowed to play any games until Dec. 1 (previously the fourth Friday in November) except for the Tipoff Classic, preseason NIT, and exhibitions against foreign touring teams.

Basketball teams will be limited to 25 (previously 28) regular-season games, counting their conference tournament as one game.

Also, teams previously could exclude from the 28-game limit an exhibition game with a touring foreign team, plus another with a club team such as Athletics in Action or the Tipoff Classic. Once every four years a tournament in Hawaii or Alaska could be exempted, as well as either the preseason NIT, a tournament in Puerto Rico, or a foreign tour.

This was changed to one exemption for any of those events every four years.

Effective next year, spring football practice will be limited to 15 sessions over 21 days (previously 20 sessions over 36 days) and contact will be allowed only during 10 of those sessions (previously 15).

Random, year-round steroid testing of football players will begin, and those who test positive will be suspended for one year. A second positive test will result in permanent suspension. Teams will be subject to sanctions (surrendering titles and revenues) for knowingly allowing a positive-tested athlete to participate in a championship or bowl.

Schools will be required to disclose graduation rates of athletes to recruits, their parents, coaches, and the NCAA.

Freshman athletes' scholarships will be expanded to cover the cost of summer school.

ASSIGNMENT 4.14

Item 1: Here are the events for Black Awareness Month programs for the Feb. 9–15 period at the University of Miami. You take the information from a press release from the university's Office of Public Affairs. The theme of the programs is "The Pain, the Pride, and the Glory." The university community, as well as the public, is invited to all events. Admissions costs are given. Put together an informational box, i.e., a story that basically itemizes events.

- Feb. 9 Gospel explosion, 8 p.m., Gusman Concert Hall, 1314 Miller Drive, Coral Gables campus. Admission, $3.
- Feb. 10 Picnic, intramural field, noon–6 p.m.
- Feb. 12–16 Events highlighting black literature, all to be announced.
- Feb. 15 Miss Black University of Miami Pageant, 7:30 p.m., Gusman Concert Hall, $3 admission.

Item 2: The University of Miami School of Music will present these events Feb. 10–14 at Gusman Concert Hall, 1314 Miller Drive, Coral Gables campus. Write an informational box on the following:

- Feb. 10 Master's recital. Giselle Elgarresta, voice, 8 p.m.
- Feb. 11 Valentine's Concert. Civic Chorale of Greater Miami, Lee Kjelson, conductor. General admission, $5; students and seniors, $3.
- Feb. 12 Master's recital. Kathleen Perry, viola, 8 p.m.
- Feb. 13 Master's recital. Rafael Elvira, violin, 8 p.m.
- Feb. 14 Guest Artist Series. Mexican Fulbright artist Gabriela Jimenez, solo percussion, 8 p.m.

For last-minute schedule changes, call MUSIKALL, 284–6477.

ASSIGNMENT 4.15

Press releases come in many forms. Most of them serve as the basis for news stories, calendar items, or PSA (public service announcements). Others, especially at small newspapers, are often printed verbatim. Some press releases provide sources for you to contact in the event you need them. In the following exercises, you will write or plan stories from a sample of these releases from the University of Miami's Office of Public Affairs and Dade County (Greater Miami) Public Schools.

Item 1: This is an example of an informational press release or source sheet. It is the beginning of hurricane season in South Florida. Read over the contacts, and then submit to your editor-instructor a list of five story ideas for hurricane season coverage. With each idea, list which university sources would be good for your story idea.

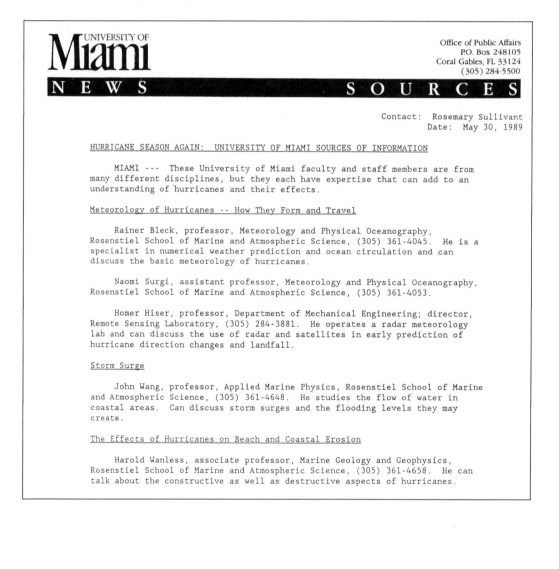

UNIVERSITY OF
Miami

Office of Public Affairs
P.O. Box 248105
Coral Gables, FL 33124
(305) 284-5500

N E W S   S O U R C E S

Contact: Rosemary Sullivant
Date: May 30, 1989

HURRICANE SEASON AGAIN: UNIVERSITY OF MIAMI SOURCES OF INFORMATION

MIAMI --- These University of Miami faculty and staff members are from many different disciplines, but they each have expertise that can add to an understanding of hurricanes and their effects.

Meteorology of Hurricanes -- How They Form and Travel

Rainer Bleck, professor, Meteorology and Physical Oceanography, Rosenstiel School of Marine and Atmospheric Science, (305) 361-4045. He is a specialist in numerical weather prediction and ocean circulation and can discuss the basic meteorology of hurricanes.

Naomi Surgi, assistant professor, Meteorology and Physical Oceanography, Rosenstiel School of Marine and Atmospheric Science, (305) 361-4053.

Homer Hiser, professor, Department of Mechanical Engineering; director, Remote Sensing Laboratory, (305) 284-3881. He operates a radar meteorology lab and can discuss the use of radar and satellites in early prediction of hurricane direction changes and landfall.

Storm Surge

John Wang, professor, Applied Marine Physics, Rosenstiel School of Marine and Atmospheric Science, (305) 361-4648. He studies the flow of water in coastal areas. Can discuss storm surges and the flooding levels they may create.

The Effects of Hurricanes on Beach and Coastal Erosion

Harold Wanless, associate professor, Marine Geology and Geophysics, Rosenstiel School of Marine and Atmospheric Science, (305) 361-4658. He can talk about the constructive as well as destructive aspects of hurricanes.

-2-

Daniel Hanes, associate professor, Applied Marine Physics, Rosenstiel School of Marine and Atmospheric Science, (305) 361-4654. Hanes studies fundamental dynamics of coastal erosion. He looks at how waves and currents affect sediments and how sediment travels to erode and to build up beaches.

Structures and Storms

John Medina, visiting professor, School of Architecture, (305) 284-3438. He can discuss the effect of storms on buildings, in particular, the stresses that high-rise buildings can withstand.

Aristides Millas, associate professor, School of Architecture, (305) 284-3438. He is a specialist on Miami's architectural history and can talk about how Miami's buildings have weathered hurricanes in the past.

Bernard LeMehaute, professor, Applied Marine Physics, Rosenstiel School of Marine and Atmospheric Science, (305) 361-4636. He can discuss the effect of hurricanes on coastal and ocean structures and describe the waves created by storms.

Michael Phang, chairman, Department of Civil Engineering, (305) 284-3391. He can talk about the durability of buildings, high rises, bridges, and roads.

History of South Florida Hurricanes

Paul George, adjunct professor, Department of History, (305) 858-6021. He can discuss the history of hurricanes in South Florida and their impact on the way we live today.

How Hurricanes Affect Children

Fred Seligman, professor, Child and Adolescent Psychiatry, (305) 547-6941. He can give advice on preparing children psychologically for hurricanes and disasters.

Effect of Hurricanes on Plants and Trees

Julia Morton, professor, Department of Biology, (305) 284-3741. Morton is an expert on Florida plants and can talk about the effect of wind and rain on vegetation.

Geography of Hurricanes

Peter Muller, professor, Department of Geography, (305) 284-4087. Muller can talk about where hurricanes occur in the world and how different cultures handle them. He can also discuss the impact of hurricanes and flooding on urban planning and development along coastlines.

How Major Institutions Plan for Disaster

Betty Baderman, news bureau chief, University of Miami Medical Center Communications, (305) 549-7304. She can describe the disaster plan for Jackson Memorial Hospital and the University of Miami Medical Center.

Christopher Dudley, director, media relations, University Relations Office, University of Miami, (305) 284-5500. He can discuss the university's main campus disaster plan.

Item 2: The following press release could be published as given or rewritten. Most large newspapers do not run press releases verbatim. Your paper doesn't want a rewrite on this item, nor will it run the information as submitted. Your editor wants you to do some checking so that you may write your own feature story about the blood drive. Read over the information. Make a list of questions (at least 10) that you would ask Andy Gollan, the contact listed on the press release.

Dr. James Fleming, Associate Superintendent • Bureau of Community & Management Services • 1450 N.E. 2 Ave., Miami, FL 33132

DADE COUNTY SCHOOLS GIVE   CONTACT: Andy Gollan
BLOOD TO RED CROSS DRIVE   376-1126

June 7, 1989

High school students, teachers, principals and administrators of the Dade County public schools donated 7,700 pints of blood to the American Red Cross this school year, representing an 18 percent increase over the previous year.

"Given the separation of each blood unit into as many as four components, Dade County senior high schools this year have directly helped more than 28,000 area patients, including trauma cases, surgical and cancer patients, burn victims and hemophiliacs, to name a few," said Deanne E. Smith, area manager for the American Red Cross.

Further information may be obtained from Smith at 326-8888.

# #

89-0248AG

Item 3: Now that you know how to get ideas from press releases, let's see you rewrite a few. You may use quotes provided in the releases. Write a six-paragraph story about the new dean of the marine school. You may use two quotes.

Office of Public Affairs
P.O. Box 248105
Coral Gables, FL 33124
(305) 284-5500

Contact: Christopher Dudley
Date: May 8, 1989

N E W S

ROSENDAHL NAMED DEAN OF UM'S ROSENSTIEL SCHOOL OF MARINE AND ATMOSPHERIC SCIENCE

CORAL GABLES -- Bruce R. Rosendahl, professor of geophysics at Duke University and director of Project PROBE, has been named dean of the University of Miami Rosenstiel School of Marine and Atmospheric Science (RSMAS), UM Executive Vice President and Provost Luis Glaser announced today.

"We are delighted that Professor Rosendahl has accepted our offer," said Glaser. "He is one of the best scholars in the field and brings with him some very important research that is critical to understanding global problems."

Rosendahl specializes in the study of rifted plate margins using exploration seismic methods, and he is an expert on the subject of continental rifting. He is the founder of Project PROBE, an ongoing geophysical study of the East African rift lakes. He has authored or co-authored more than 100 scientific publications. To continue his research at RSMAS, Rosendahl will occupy the Lewis G. Weeks Chair in Geology, which was established in 1987 by former trustee Marta Weeks in memory of her father-in-law.

"I am pleased to be going to a school with such an outstanding reputation and will work to continue to improve its quality and international standing. We would like to see RSMAS in the very forefront of marine and atmospheric research," said Rosendahl.

The appointment of Rosendahl culminates a search for a permanent dean for RSMAS since the departure of Alan Berman more than two years ago. Geology Professor Christopher G.A. Harrison has served as interim dean during that time.

-more-

Rosendahl/2

"We are thankful to Professor Harrison for his able stewardship of the school during a very difficult time," said Glaser. "The university owes him a debt of gratitude."

Rosendahl's academic credentials include B.S. and M.S. degrees in geology and geophysics from the Hawaii Institute of Geophysics at the University of Hawaii. He has a Ph.D. in earth sciences from Scripps Institute of Oceanography at the University of California, San Diego.

Professor Rosendahl is the chairman of the board, director, and/or chief operating officer of several companies he has helped form. He has consulted for most of the major international petroleum companies, the World Bank, and several foreign governments.

Though Rosendahl officially assumes his duties on July 1, he will begin moving his operation, including Project PROBE, to Miami immediately.

-30-

Editor's Note: Dr. Glaser can be reached at (305) 284-3356 and Dr. Rosendahl may be reached at (919) 684-6715.

Item 4: Rewrite the following press release, using as much information as you want. The emphasis of this assignment is to test your ability to present the information provided in your own words. (Hint: Check spelling on the name of the scholarship at your campus library.)

Dr. James Fleming, Associate Superintendent • Bureau of Community & Management Services • 1450 N.E. 2 Ave., Miami, FL 33132

TWO DADE SENIORS ARE RUNNERS UP IN LIONEL RITCHIE SCHOLARSHIP FUND

CONTACT: Hilda Diaz
376-1126

June 8, 1989

Two Dade County Public School students have been named runners up in the Lionel Ritchie Scholarship Fund.

Bertha Fertil, a senior at Miami Edison Senior High School, was first runner up and will receive a $2,000 scholarship. Tonda Davis, a senior at Miami Jackson Senior High School, was third runner up and will receive a $500 scholarship. Bertha will attend Cornell University and Tonda is deciding between Barry University and the University of Miami.

The Lionel Ritchie Scholarship Fund is a national competition which awards money to at-risk students who stay in high school and graduate. The students are helped by the Private Industry Council which provides dropout prevention services in 13 of Dade County's public high schools.

Further information may be obtained from Harriet Spivak, Private Industry Council, at 594-7615.

# #

89-0252HD

Item 5: Press releases are sometimes full stories reported and written by institutional or organization staffs. This press release on food poisoning is much too long for your paper. You have been asked to make it into a brief of no more than five paragraphs. You may also use the quotes provided. In this assignment, you must use the skill you are learning to develop in this chapter: organization.

UNIVERSITY OF

Miami

FEATURES

Office of Public Affairs
P.O. Box 248105
Coral Gables, FL 33124
(305) 284-5500

The Most Common Food Poisoning: To: Food Editor or
A Ciguatera Primer   Science Editor

The most commonly reported food poisoning is not salmonella or botulism or amoebic dysentery but ciguatera--found in the flesh of tropical reef fish. More than 400 species, sold across much of the United States, have been implicated as carriers.

Fish is ten times more likely to give you food poisoning than beef, seven times more than chicken, six times more than pork, according to Ellen Haas of Public Voice for Food and Health Policy.

At the same time, fish consumption is up 20 percent since 1980. The average American eats more than 15 pounds per year.

Ciguatera can be an extremely debilitating disease.

Symptoms usually begin within an hour of eating the fish. They include nausea, vomiting, stomach cramps and sometimes diarrhea. Then they get worse. Many experience a crawly, tingly or electric-shocklike sensation around the lips, tongue, throat, fingers and toes, often followed by severe itching all over the body and a rash or blisters. Hot objects may feel icy, cold objects feel hot to the touch. The victim has severe headaches, dizziness and lack of coordination. There is pain in the muscles, joints and bones. The teeth may feel loose. Fatigue sets in. The victim may be bedridden for days, weeks, months or, occasionally, for years.

The symptoms last for an average of six to 18 months but they can persist for as long as 25 years. An occasional side effect is paranoia.

—more—

Ciguatera/Pg. 2

There is no known test for the detection of ciguatera in fish. There is no known preventative. There is no known cure. Only a handful of doctors--in South Florida and Hawaii--can recognize ciguatera. In the rest of the country many--perhaps most--have never heard of it. None can do anything for the victim except treat the symptoms. Acute episodes are sometimes treated with mannitol, an artificial sugar.

Nobody knows how many cases of ciguatera occur in the U.S. every year-- unrecognized, unreported, untreated, uncured. The only way to prevent ciguatera is to understand it and, when buying fish, know exactly what you are buying.

But that isn't easy, says Don de Sylva of the University of Miami's Rosenstiel School of Marine and Atmospheric Science (RSMAS), who has studied ciguatera since the 1950s.

To understand why, you must know what's been learned about ciguatera itself. Scientists believe the malady is caused by micro-organisms called dinoflagellates that live on tropical coral reefs. Small fish eat them. Larger fish eat the smaller fish, the toxin becoming ever more concentrated as it moves up the food chain.

Unfortunately, says RSMAS's Daniel G. Baden, who studies the dinoflagellates, addressing the consumer of reef fish: "You are the end of the food chain."

The fishes most likely to carry ciguatoxin are the large, predatory reef fish. These include the barracudas, grouper, snappers, jacks, mackerels, parrotfish, surgeonfish and wrasse families. But within these families, not all species carry ciguatoxin.

Of the Caribbean fish, those thought to be safe include Nassau grouper and red grouper, the vermillion snapper and yellowtail snapper. True red

-more-

Ciguatera/Pg. 3

snapper is believed to be safe--but many other red-colored snapper-like fish
are sold under that name, and may not be safe.

Matters are even more complicated.

Within a given species most individual fish may be safe, while a few-
especially the largest-may be toxic.

Toxicity most often depends on the fish's point of origin--the particular
reef on which it has fed, says de Sylva, who is studying the location of safe
and toxic reefs in the Caribbean. Some are safe, he says, and others toxic.

This leaves the fish consumer with a problem.

There is simply no way to tell if a particular fish--caught or bought--is
toxic without sensitive, expensive chemical analysis--which destroys the fish.
The toxins cannot be tasted. No amount of washing, freezing, cooking,
marinating, smoking or irradiating will render them harmless.

Folk assays have evolved in the Caribbean, whose people have known for
centuries that some fish are poisonous. Some believe that a silver coin cooked
with the fish will turn black if the fish is toxic. Others are convinced that
flies will not land on a toxic fish, that ants will not feed on a toxic fish,
or that the teeth of a toxic barracuda will be dark at the root, or that a
toxic fish is weakened by the dinoflagellate and does not fight well when
hooked.

The trouble with these home tests, de Sylva says, is that none of them
works.

Then how do you tell what fish is safe to eat?

The best way to avoid ciguatera, de Sylva says, is to avoid the large,
predatory fish from tropical coral reef areas. "Remember that smaller
specimens in Florida may usually be eaten without harm," he says.

"Smaller" means three to five pounds in snapper or hogfish, 10 pounds for

-more-

Ciguatera/Pg. 4

grouper in Florida. Never, he says, eat a barracuda over three pounds.

Any freshwater fish is safe. So is any saltwater fish that does not feed on the reefs. These include tuna, wahoo, swordfish, marlin, dolphin. Also safe are inshore and estuarine fish such as snook, redfish, sea trout, drum, croaker, whiting, mullet, sheepshead, flounder and grunt. Other safe fish, he says, are sailfish, Spanish mackerel, small king mackerel and yellowtail snapper.

In addition, non-migratory snapper and grouper caught in the Gulf of Mexico are safe, since the Gulf has virtually no coral reefs to shelter the toxin.

But how do you tell what fish you are buying?

"If you buy whole fish," de Sylva says, "you can tell what it is, of course, if you know fish. Even that isn't always easy. There are 19 species of snapper in the Caribbean, for example. "But if it isn't whole, you usually have no idea. I've been eating fish all my life and, frankly, 1 can't tell them apart if it's a large filet cut into smaller pieces. Customers can be duped easily."

Recently, consumer groups have called for stricter fish inspection and closer attention to accurate identification and labelling.

It isn't going to be easy. But, says de Sylva and other experts, it is overdue. "Deception is rampant in fish sales," he says.

"In 99 percent of the fish we eat, we don't know what they are and it doesn't really matter. In one percent, it does."

#
                                    --Jack McClintock

Item 6: Here is another story that is ready to publish in your newspaper. Your editor at a small newspaper likes the story and finds it very appropriate for the community, which has a large elderly population. You've been asked to tighten the story and do some rewriting. Use your judgment and submit a good story, incorporating the seven bullet items. One thing, however, don't start your story with a quote.

FEATURES

Office of Public Affairs
P.O. Box 248105
Coral Gables, FL 33124
(305) 284-5500

How to Prevent   To: Health/Medicine Editor
Drug Misuse by Elderly

"Drug misuse by the elderly has been discussed for 10 years, but there's been little progress," says Dr. Patricia Barry, associate professor of clinical medicine, University of Miami School of Medicine.

The problem is more serious than many have believed, Barry says.

"There are more treatment complications in elderly patients than in younger patients," she says, "and drugs are the most important cause. There's a three- to seven-times greater chance of adverse drug reactions in an elderly patient."

In the United States, the elderly comprise 11 percent of the population but they consume 25 percent of the drugs. And among those over 65, 25 to 50 percent of patients are "non-compliant"--either do not take their drugs or take them improperly or unsafely.

Medical professionals, Barry says, must better understand the risk factors, recognize the problem medications and manage drugs appropriately. In one recent study, 36 percent of health problems arising from drug misuse were blamed on the doctor.

But the problem is not so simple. Administering drugs for the elderly is complicated by the patient's often diminished reserves of health and the likelihood of more than one illness, which increases the chances of multiple drugs interacting with dangerous side effects.

In addition, patients may omit taking drugs, or take the wrong drugs, or take prescription drugs in combination with over-the-counter drugs whose

-more-

Drugs/Pg. 2

strength they underestimate, or take drugs prescribed by more than one physician. Some patients may take drugs carelessly or accidentally or in hazardous, self-prescribed combinations--polypharmacy or "brown bag syndrome," some physicians call it.

Certain diseases increase risk. "Decreased liver function limits the detoxifying function," for instance, Barry says. Malnutrition, kidney insufficiency or heart insufficiency can also make a patient vulnerable.

The aging process itself creates risk factors. "In older people, drugs are absorbed the same," Barry says, "but the elderly store them longer in body fat, resulting in drugs staying around longer."

Sensory loss may cause problems in hearing instructions or reading labels. Cognitive capacity may be reduced.

Barry says doctors, nurses and patients themselves could profit by being more watchful for toxic reactions and by assuming less. "Just because the patient has been taking a drug for a long time doesn't mean there's no toxic reaction."

Among the most commonly troublesome drugs are the anticholinergics. These include many antidepressants, antipsychotics, anti-Parkinson drugs, and some over-the-counter drugs. They are useful, Barry says, "but they have a group of side effects: urinary retention, constipation, dry mouth, and the possibility of mental confusion."

In elderly patients, such drugs even taken at night may be retained into the next day and cause trouble. The same is true of sleeping pills.

"We've seen many elderly people with increasing mental confusion because of over-the-counter cold medicines. Many don't consider these to be real drugs. But they are."   —more—

Drugs/Pg. 3

Many of the antiarrhythmic heart drugs can be dangerous, too. Barry calls them a Pandora's box. "In some, the toxic dose is very close to the therapeutic dose." Such drugs require careful monitoring.

The diuretics can also have some bad effects, including fluid depletion, electrolyte depletion, urinary incontinence. "Even these are not totally benign drugs."

Most problems, Barry says, are "preventable by education." She offers some general guidelines for patients and doctors.

Patients should take drugs only as prescribed and should ask about possible side effects. They should tell their doctor about other drugs they are taking, including over-the-counter drugs.

Doctors should stick to the drugs with the least side effects. "Use the equally effective but less toxic drug in the same category," she says. "Not doing that is the most common prescription error."

Beyond that:

*   Stop non-essential medications.

*   Review indications for drugs--is the drug still necessary?

*   Review evidence of the drug's effectiveness--is it helping?

*   Initiate therapy one drug at a time.

*   Monitor and assess dosage carefully.

*   Monitor effects and toxicity closely.

*   When there's trouble, always consider drugs as a possible cause.

And when in doubt, she says, stop the medication and observe the patient.

                                        #
                                                --Jack McClintock

Item 7: Write a 15-second public service announcement based on the following information:

The University of Miami will offer two mini-semesters this summer from May through July. The courses will be for credit and non-credit. Classes, which range from sailing to calculus are for college students and adults. For further information, call the university's summer session hotline: 284–4000. Outside of Miami, call 1–800–626–7173.

Item 8: Write a 30-second public service announcement based on the following information:

A series of intensive, one-week courses will be offered by the University of Miami to help state-certified teachers renew or extend their teaching certificates. Courses begin in the middle of June and are open to all Florida teachers. Full-time teachers are eligible to receive a 50 percent discount. For more information on this master educator series for teachers, call toll-free: 1–800–626–7173.

5 Revising: Editing, Rewriting, Updating

ASSIGNMENT 5.1

Tape a local radio newscast lead story. Then tape the same news story on the next newscast, which is aired on the same station. How are stories in the second newscast updated and revised from the first to the second newscast? How much time has elapsed between newscasts?

ASSIGNMENT 5.2

Take one of your own news stories that you have recently written. Count the length in words and pages, or if it is a script, in minutes and seconds. Now rewrite your story, cutting the length of the original story in half. Can you do it? What was eliminated? Why?

ASSIGNMENT 5.3

The next time you encounter a grammar problem in preparing a story, call one of the grammar hotlines listed in chapter 5 in the text. Or, if your own campus has one, visit it to meet with an adviser to discuss the problem.

What did you learn?

ASSIGNMENT 5.4

After you have written and self-edited one of your writing assignments, ask someone else to edit it. What does this person see in your story that you may have missed?

ASSIGNMENT 5.5

Ask your instructor to let you watch him or her grade, and even edit, your next writing assignment. Discuss what he or she does and why.

ASSIGNMENT 5.6

Identify and edit the cliches out of the following sentences.

1. The councilman, almost like a bolt from the blue, stormed into the meeting and announced his resignation.

2. It was important for the school superintendent to get the new year off on the right foot.

3. The mayor's press secretary said she wanted to nip in the bud any controversy over the budget process.

4. Pain and suffering are inextricably linked.

5. For the city's unemployed youth, the handwriting is on the wall: a long hot summer could mean an increase in gang activity.

6. The new chief executive officer's life had become a rags-to-riches story.

7. The crowd voiced its approval of the Soviet dissident's speech.

8. The sheriff vowed he would leave no stone unturned in his efforts to locate the suspect.

9. Cool as a cucumber, the mayor announced that 1,000 city employees would be laid off due to budget cuts.

10. The residents come from all walks of life—from maintenance workers to managers.

ASSIGNMENT 5.7

Look for holes, clutter, redundancy, cliches, and word usage errors in the following original student essays. Edit these stories with those points in mind. These are original student stories.

Item 1:

Recently sworn in an as the City of South Miami's first female mayor, Cathy McCann said that she still believes in the principle that she told her high school government students 20 years ago: "You get out of the government what you put into it."

This principle might explain McCann's widespread involvement with city government since she moved to South Miami almost 20 years ago. She spent a total of 10 years on the City Commission, four of which she acted as vice mayor.

McCann received 63 percent of the vote on Feb. 13 as opposed to 37 percent for opponent Danny Brown.

McCann, born in 1933, currently resides at 5820 SW 87th St., near Dante Fascell Park. She said that she especially likes South Miami for its ability to retain the image of a small town while being located so close to the city of Miami and Miami International Airport.

"In 1990, I see South Miami as a great place to live," she said.

McCann is married to Peter, who is employed by what she said is "an international corporation." While her husband has been supportive of her past political activities, she said that this was the first campaign he was "enthusiastic about."

McCann has three grown children, two daughters, and one son. One of her daughters is considering moving back to South Miami. McCann said many young people are returning to South Miami, where they grew up, because of its small-town nature and proximity to downtown Miami.

McCann herself is originally from Maine and received a BA from Kalamazoo College in Michigan. She taught high school for several years, and became involved in politics after moving to South Miami.

McCann said she never planned to become so politically active, but several years ago, a situation around her home motivated her to do so.

At the time, McCann had open land surrounding her home. When the land was marked for development, she said, the zoning laws were challenged, and she was afraid that the area would be developed inappropriately. Thus, she became politically active.

"I needed to make a difference," she said.

Since her start in politics, McCann has been a member of several city boards and committees: the Public Safety Committee; the Zoning Task Force, of which she was chairman; the Signage Committee; the Comprehensive Plan Review Committee, chairman; the South Miami Action Committee, founding member; and she was also chairman of the Commercial Development Committee.

Along with these activities, McCann has been president of the South Miami Homeowners Association and a member of the board of directors for the Dade League of Cities.

Despite her success in city government, McCann said that it is still difficult for her to secure the male vote. She said that her campaign image is very important to male voters.

"I try to be firm without being termed an aggressive broad," she said.

McCann is a member of the First United Methodist Church of South Miami, and said that she has been an active member of the congregation. According to her campaign literature, McCann has also been involved in Girl Scouts, USA, the Riviera Day Care Center and the PTA. She is a registered Republican.

Aside from these aspects of her personal life, McCann said that there is one important occurrence that stands out in her mind: her fight with breast cancer. She said that she believes it to be a part of her life that other women should know about.

McCann said that another subject she feels strongly about is abortion. Personally, she is pro-choice, and she said that abortion is an issue that should not be handled on a city government level. She also said that while politicians tried to avoid the issue in the past, it is is necessary for today's public figures to take a definite stand, as she has done.

McCann said that she also has very definite opinions on the subjects of drugs and crime.

"Crime and drugs are always a problem," she said. "I don't know the answer."

What she does know, she said, is that the proper steps are not being taken. She said that too much emphasis is being placed on punishment, rather than rehabilitation, and that more programs need to be focused on the young people at risk in the community—the potential trouble makers.

She wants to look into the positive programs that stop young people from getting involved in crime in the first place, she said.

"We need to get to the root of the problem," she said.

One final issue McCann focuses on is that of recycling. She said that it is her goal to reduce trash by 30 percent in the next few years. In order to do this, she said, she wants to start a paper, glass and aluminum recycling program this month. McCann also said that she started Dade County's first newspaper recycling program in 1974. While the theory of such a widespread recycling program may appeal to the city as whole, she said, making it work will be difficult.

"It is amazing how many people give lip service to recycling," she said, and "when it comes right down to actually recycling, nobody wants to do it."

McCann conducted a "door-to-door" type campaign for the recent election. She said that she did not ask for money from anyone, which she said is "distasteful," and assured donors that their money did not guarantee political favors. McCann estimates that she raised $4,000–$5,000, and she said that she ran a simple campaign without a public relations person.

"The voters should see you as yourself," she said. "and know that you care."

Cathy McCann, South Miami's first female mayor, speaks out strongly on these and other issues and carries to her office much political experience and a taste for Nicaraguan food. She is also an active member of her community whose recent 63 percent to 37 percent victory over opponent Danny Brown shows the city's support of her in this non-partisan election.

Item 2:

Ask students and instructors about registration they will tell you that closed or cancelled classes are more and more becoming part of the registration procedure.

Professor Francois Lejeune of the School of Architecture announced his new class, "The Stage or Architecture," in the Spring schedule. He was told earlier this month to cancel his class because there were too few students who had registered by January.

"I needed 12 registered students to be allowed to teach, and only 7 were interested in the theme of the class." he said.

"When they are told that a class is closed, students first react by complaining," said Lejeune. "But, they have to realize that more students, let us say, 20 instead of 16 in a class, may affect the quality of the lessons. That's probably why teachers are reluctant to ask for an authorization to accept more students. We have less time to pay attention to the progress of each of them.

"But on the other hand, you cannot open a new class with only an extra of four students."

Tom Prince, a freshman in the math department took the "closed class problem" philosophically: "Twice the computer told me the English class that I wanted to get was closed. But it was not really a problem. You always have the possibility to adjust your schedule."

"I know some students who had to rework their schedules," said John Williams, a freshman music major, "but I did not." Williams said that transferred students are more likely to face that situation, because they have to go through administrative procedures that can delay their registration.

George Punchong, a biology student who transferred from Boston University this semester, had no trouble setting his schedule; but he heard that "other transferred students did."

"I guess I did not have that problem, because my classes are not that popular." said Elena Martinez, who is graduating in psychology major.

Indeed, required classes for first-year students, such as English 105 or English 106, are rapidly closed, because of the large number of students who have to register. "But the decision to close a class is beyond the control of the department," said the secretary of the English department. "Such a decision is taken by the office of the executive vice president and provost," she said.

However, as Lejeune pointed out earlier the early registration is not the best solution to avoid a closed class.

Neither is the opening of new classes; rather, it is even a short term, and a double-edged solution. "Because all these part-time positions might be closing the following semester, if the total number of students drops unexpectedly.

Item 3:

It is a frequent sight around the University of Miami campus during registration to see scores of frustrated students desperately adjusting and readjusting their schedules because a class they planned to take was full.

Not only do students have to wait in line for up to an hour, they find that by the time they get to the computer, the waiting was the easy part.

"I spent three days begging for signatures needed for an override because the classes I wanted were full to allocation," said junior accounting major John Pierini. "If you want the classes, you have to work at it. Some people don't, they just give up."

When a class is closed due to allocation, a student may find himself spending an entire afternoon travelling from building to building and professor to professor to get the signatures needed for an override. Even this effort is sometimes useless for reasons out of the student's or professor's control.

"The problem with closed sections involves many things," said Katharine Thompson, manager of the Division of Registration. "Sometimes there just aren't any seats available, which neither a professor or student can change."

"I find that it is very rare that a student is able to register for the sections they want, but they always can get into another section of the same class," said Thompson.

This was not the case of Regina Edwards, a sophomore motion pictures major, when the class she wanted offered only one section. She was admitted to the desired class only after a few heated conversations between herself and the film department.

"Yes, I got angry," said Edwards. "It was a class I needed to take to graduate on time. I mean, we pay our tuition, I think we should be entitled to take the classes we want."

As in Edwards' case some students have to take classes specifically required for their major. This problem is commonplace with communication students since each communication major has a track of classes that must be taken in order. If a student can't take a class a certain semester he gets off track and won't graduate on time.

Isabelle Chamberet, a senior public relations major, recalls her problem with a closed class that would inhibit her from graduating on time.

"It's so frustrating telling someone you can't graduate on time without that class and they still tell you 'no'. I ended up convincing the Dean of the School of Communication to convince the professor to let me in. They treat us like criminals. It's not fair."

Exactly what is fair? One may argue that it is not fair that honor students and athletes are allowed to register before anyone else, thus guaranteeing their choice of classes. This university policy could be looked at as form of discrimination.

One adamant honor student was Karl Stewart, a junior international studies major.

"I think it's fair to let us register early," said Stewart. "We've worked hard to become honor students, we deserve the privilege that goes with it. But I have to admit there really is no justifiable reason in letting us."

As fair or unfair as the system is, some students actually hit the jackpot with an early registration appointment while others will continue to rework schedules, track down professors for signatures, and spend countless hours in lines praying they will end up with a half-way decent schedule.

Not all registrars and professors are heartless, however, as they can be coaxed into changing their minds with a lot of time and patience and maybe just a little ranting and raving. After all, as Thompson said, "I've never heard any complaints from students."

ASSIGNMENT 5.8

The following sentences, all taken from student publications, contain clutter, redundancies, and cliches. Clean them up.

1. Both Browne and Vitali say they hope this election does not turn into a war between minorities and Greeks, but they cannot ignore how closely the numbers run.

2. All proceeds from sales will go to the feeding of the animals and the student education program, he said.

3. Detectives from the UW police department are in the process of verifying the identities of student protesters who participated in the flag-burning incident Monday in Red Square.

4. The Gallup organization conducted a similar survey in 1986 to test 17-year-olds for their knowledge of history and literature. In fact, more than one-third of the questions on the test for college seniors were just recycled questions from the 17-year-olds' test.

5. Michener ended the evening by saying the life of a writer is rewarding but not as easy as some people think.

6. Reed, a senior majoring in communication representing Sigma Delta Tau sorority, and 13 other finalists competed in the Brenda Smith-Tucker Memorial Miss University of Miami Scholarship pageant.

7. Norman said that although they do not know how many potential students have actually applied, more than 1,200 applications and program catalogs have been sent out as of last week.

8. He said that although there is nothing wrong with the idea, it may not really be needed.

9. Anderson's bill may not even get a hearing in the House.

10. Susi said she will seek the aid of Dr. Craig Ullom, director of the University Center and student life who also serves as adviser to the Student Government, to be sure of the correct course of action.

ASSIGNMENT 5.9

The following sentences contain grammatical and other errors. Identify and fix.

1. Everyone of us have been confronted with that dilemma.
2. Whom should get the honor of welcoming the mayor?
3. The governor insisted that the new appointees prioritize their concerns.
4. She was unable to get through the work that piled up on her desk.
5. Stating that she would be in a better mood Monday, the meeting was cancelled.
6. They will happily go to the award banquet.
7. The president asked to lay down for a few minutes.
8. If she was the right candidate, he would have endorsed her a long time ago.
9. Although he is young and inexperienced, he sings just as a professional.
10. Leave sleeping dogs lay.

ASSIGNMENT 5.10

The following sentences contain word usage errors. Identify and correct. (There are a couple of sentences that have no errors.)

1. The affect of the decision will be pervasive.
2. The agenda are ready for perusal.
3. The illusion to Shakespeare was misunderstood by the readers.
4. Just between you and I, there's no point in going to the program.
5. Expecting that more than five would arrive, she prepared a meal for 10.
6. An average of 20 people is always there.
7. He said he felt bad about the decision.
8. Stand here besides me.
9. He can't hardly get out of bed.
10. The car collided into the tree.
11. They agreed to pursue the issue farther.
12. He had less votes than his challenger.
13. Staff reductions, fewer promotions and a pay freeze compromise the mayor's budget proposal.
14. The celebrants raced onto the field to congratulate the winning team.
15. Presently, six people serve on the board.
16. The sanguine disposition of the clown drew applause and laughter.
17. While the water was warm at noon, it was considerably cooler at 6 p.m.
18. He compared apartheid in South Africa to racism in the United States.
19. She convinced him to read the articles.
20. He contrasted the pro-life debate with the pro-choice platform.

ASSIGNMENT 5.11

Edit the following published articles. Look for holes, improper word usage, cliches, clutter, redundancy, and grammar problems.

Item 1:

NEWSPAPER NAME: *The Central Florida Future*, University of Central Florida
DATE: Thursday, January 25, 1990
VOL. 22, NO. 37
HEADLINE: Children may have new day care this fall
PAGES: 1, 4

Student leaders and administrators are taking the first tentative steps to start a drop-off day care program at UCF by the fall.

The Creative School for Children offers regular, programmed day care for the children of students, faculty, and staff members. But the school has a long waiting list, and students who only need the service occasionally have had to find another option. These are the people the drop-off day care would serve.

"We're looking to fit the needs of the non-traditional student," said Student Government Chief of Staff Jeff Laing. "It will be for the students taking one or two classes.

"They can drop off their children, go to class and then pick them up."

Those working on the project are not sure how many students would take advantage of it, but early response has been positive.

Within a few days of a story about the project in *The Orlando Sentinel*, Laing received several calls from interested students.

"They wanted to sign up already," Laing said.

According to a survey done this fall of 449 evening students, 11 percent would take advantage of evening day care if UCF offered it for a nominal fee. Most students, 81 percent, said the question was not applicable to them, and 8 percent said they would not use drop-off evening day care, according to Jimmy Watson, director of student information and evening/weekend services.

If those numbers hold true for the rest of UCF's 10,000-student evening population, the service would get plenty of use. UCF defines an evening student as anyone taking at least one class starting at 5 p.m. or later.

About 2,500 students on the main campus take no day classes at all.

Laing estimates that the project's start-up will require about $50,000 in student government funds, which come from the tuition each student pays. The costs are still being figured, but the money would go toward new personnel, equipment and, possibly, facilities for the Creative School, which would be running the program.

"It's almost like a repeat of history," said Dolores Burghard, director of the Creative School, "because they're the ones that got us started.

Student government paid to set up the Creative School in 1976 and subsidized it for several years until it began making money. The new project would probably be similarly supported.

Burghard has been working with student government leaders to estimate the cost of the drop-off service. She is optimistic about its prospects.

"It will probably start off slow until people find out about it and then it will grow," she said.

Student body President Fred Schmidt agreed.

He said the people working on the project still have a lot of homework to do, but, he added, "I think it's almost 100 percent that something will materialize by this fall."

Reprinted with the permission of the Florida Southern College *Southern.*

Item 2:

NEWSPAPER NAME: *The Southern,* Florida Southern College
DATE: Friday, February 9, 1990
VOL. 104, NO. 3
HEADLINE: 'Pal Program' reaches children needing a friend
PAGES: 1, 8

Several local college students are playing the role of "big buddy" in their spare time to help underprivileged children get a better chance at life.

Through a new program initiated by the Central Avenue Elementary School in Lakeland, children from low socioeconomic backgrounds are seeing what potential gifts life can bring when someone is willing to show them the way.

The Pal Program helps children in kindergarten through 6th grade who, because of poor home environments, are likely to become dropouts. Currently, 20 students from South Eastern College and one from FSC are donating an hour of their time a week to visit with a couple of children to become a friend, tutor, and role model.

"These are children who are low in skills and come from deprived homes," said Sherrie Nickell, founder of the program. "When the students come to visit, it gives them something to look forward to—a good taste of things to come."

Nickell said she began the program last semester with SEC and got such a good response that she decided to do it again this semester.

"We are trying to encourage the children by providing them with a positive role model. It's a support kind of thing," said Nickell.

FSC sophomore Joy Melner joined the program this semester and said it is self-rewarding to be able to act as a motivator.

"It's something stable in their lives," said the Early Childhood and Elementary Education major. "At home they can't talk to their parents because they do not care. The program has made me aware of their problems at home—the kids need someone there to talk to."

"The student involvement in the community caught the attention of FSC President Robert A. Davis, who has begun to see how else FSC students can become civically responsible," said Lon Turner, assistant to the Dean of Students.

"We are trying to make our students more aware of their civic responsibilities," said Turner. "We want to organize a central program where we can foster this type of program." Turner said many top businesses look favorably at student involvement in the community when they are hiring. "It can make you stand out from other applicants," he said.

Anyone interested in donating an hour a week as a "big buddy" should contact Lon Turner, extension 4206.

6 News Story Research

Today's library assignment is to find the answers to the following questions. Use whatever references (and people for that matter) you find necessary to get the answers. Photocopies of answers from books will save time if you want to use them instead of writing down information. Work alone, too—it will help you learn the reference materials.

1. Describe the Great Seal of the State of Florida.

2. In what year was Kentucky's first constitution drafted?

3. What percent of the State of California is owned by the federal government?

4. What is the zip code for Louisville, Tennessee?

5. How far is the highway mileage from Bradenton, Florida, to Apalachicola, Florida?

6. When was Cook County, Illinois, established? For whom is it named?

7. Who is president of the Massachusetts Senate?

8. What county in Washington state is the largest in terms of square miles? How does your school's county size compare?

9. On what exact date did the first Mariel refugees land at Key West, Fla., in 1980?

10. What is the current circulation of *National Geographic*?

11. Name the managing editor of *The New York Times*.

12. Geographically, where is Midway, Kentucky? (Be precise—you are describing it in a story).

13. What is the title, office address, office telephone number, and home address of Mr. Richard Oleszewski, an attorney who works for the Joint Committee on Printing in the U.S. Congress in Washington, D.C.?

14. Who is Marjory Stoneman Douglas and what was the title of her best known book? When was she born?

15. Where (what location) did Abraham Lincoln die?

ASSIGNMENT 6.2

Call your local newspaper or favorite television station to arrange a visit to its news library. If you contact a news librarian, he or she will explain how the librarians assist news writers and reporters in preparing their stories.

ASSIGNMENT 6.3

Visit your campus library and ask about electronic data base search capabilities. One or more librarians may be responsible for these services, so find out whom you should contact. Ask how you can use the services in your classwork. For one of your next assignments, try a search to help you find background material on the subject.

ASSIGNMENT 6.4

Read the cover story in this week's *Newsweek, Time,* or *U.S. News & World Report*. What research is apparent from reading this article? What sources did the writers use in addition to interviews? Can you think of additional reference sources for the story? What about experts in your own community who might have contributed information or opinions?

ASSIGNMENT 6.5

Telephone a local journalist and ask him or her to describe to you the reference books he or she most often uses on the job. How are these useful? How does he or she use them?

ASSIGNMENT 6.6

Write a profile on a university professor or sports coach. This profile will be based more on observation than investigation, although both are crucial in a good story. Arrange to interview the professor ONLY after you have spent time observing the professor in his/her working environment (classroom, research lab, or field). You must also interview other people with whom this person interacts (students, other professors, administrators, or office workers).

ASSIGNMENT 6.7

Visit a local museum, art gallery, or library exhibit. Take notes on the exhibit. Be able to describe for your readers what the exhibit encompasses, i.e., interesting pieces, history, trivia. Observe others as they pass through the exhibit. What are their reactions?

Finally, interview some of the visitors, exhibit coordinators, or museum personnel about the exhibit. Make sure you have the basic information to go along with your observation (length of exhibit, number of pieces, and so forth). Have fun with this feature story. It should be no longer than three pages.

ASSIGNMENT 6.8

Ask a professor (perhaps the same one you selected in Assignment 6.6) or administrator for a copy of his/her resume or curriculum vitae. This may also be obtained from the professor's academic department or through the campus media relations department. This is easier to get at public colleges than private, but make the attempt.

Professors, like any one else, may be reluctant to give this information to a student. Explain that you are using the resume for a class assignment on incorporating background information into a news story. Once you get the resume, it will be your job to verify the following: all entries under academic background (undergraduate and up), employment background, and published works. If the resume is lengthy, select no fewer than a total of 20 items to check. Bring your report to class, including any discrepancies you may have found.

ASSIGNMENT 6.9

Obtain a copy of *The New York Times, The Washington Post,* or the local newspaper of your hometown for the day you were born. You can probably find these on microfilm in your campus library.

What were the main news stories of the day (national, international, local if you have the paper from your city)? What was happening on the sports page? What was the weather like that day?

Now, profile your year of birth. Who was president, governor, representatives in Congress? Who was mayor of your city? Who was president of the local public school board? What was the nation's and your state's per capita income? What was the national and state unemployment rate? What books were on the best seller list? What were the popular hit records, movies, and Broadway plays?

ASSIGNMENT 6.10

Research a famous living personality. Information should be biographical, taken from the sources mentioned in the textbook for this chapter. In addition, using the *Reader's Guide to Periodical Literature,* and a newspaper index, include the latest information you can find (to the day, week, or month).

ASSIGNMENT 6.11

Draw some conclusions about marriage laws in the United States based on listings available in many common reference books, such as the most recent edition of *The World Almanac and Book of Facts*. You can get a current copy of this book at most libraries and bookstores.

Look under "marriage laws" of the 50 states of the U.S. Next, focus on where your state (place of birth, or if you are not from the United States, the state where you currently reside) stands in relation to other states.

Now, get comments from clergy, state officials, marriage counselors, and couples planning to wed. Write a story.

ASSIGNMENT 6.12

Write a short story—a "brite"—about the original names of some noted personalities. Use information based on listings available in many common reference books such as the most recent edition of *The World Almanac and Book of Facts*. You can get a current copy of this book at most libraries and bookstores. Look under a subject title such as "noted personalities" or "original names of entertainers."

Pick your favorites. Of course, you must do some research about their careers and background to fill out the story. You may focus on one entertainer while mentioning some of the original names of others, or you may do a compilation of several.

ASSIGNMENT 6.13

Write a story about the interesting data you gather from a reference book containing information about bachelor's degrees. Use information based on listings available in many common reference books such as the most recent edition of *The World Almanac and Book of Facts* or information published by the U.S. Department of Education. You can get a current copy of *The World Almanac and Book of Facts* at most libraries and bookstores.

Look under "bachelor's degrees conferred" or "education." Look at the difference, for example, in education degrees in 1970 and 1985. Look at the increase in business degrees over the same period.

How do these findings compare with degrees granted by your college or university?

7 | Law and Ethics in News Writing

ASSIGNMENT 7.1

Go to the school library and ask a reference librarian to help you find a copy of your state's libel and privacy statutes. Read them and prepare a summary of the limitations on news writing and reporting that may exist.

ASSIGNMENT 7.2

At your school's library, research your state's open meetings and open records statutes. What do the laws specifically include and exclude?

After reading the laws, check for any specific interpretations of the law by contacting the nearest office of the state attorney general for a current copy of rulings.

ASSIGNMENT 7.3

Call a local newspaper editor and ask if the newspaper has a code of ethics. Or call one of your local television stations to determine if a code of ethics exists. Request a copy. When you get it, check to see how this code differs from those of the Society of Professional Journalists, American Society of Newspaper Editors, and the Radio-Television News Directors Association, reprinted in Appendices A, B, and C of the textbook.

ASSIGNMENT 7.4

With your instructor's assistance, invite a local attorney who specializes in mass media law to speak to your class. Ask your visitor to discuss libel and privacy laws in your state.

ASSIGNMENT 7.5

College journalists are faced with ethical problems more often than they may believe. The following paragraphs represent hypothetical cases, but they resemble situations that have occurred at university or college news media newsrooms. How would you resolve each one? Write a one- or two-paragraph discussion on each one using Roy Peter Clark's model for ethical thinking discussed in Chapter 7 of the textbook as the basis for your analysis.

1. A member of the student newspaper sports department staff is also a member of the Rugby Club on campus. The sports editor has assigned this student to cover the team because he is a member and because he travels with the team and can report from the road. Is this a conflict of interest? What happens when you consider budget limitations for travel to cover minor sports teams?

2. A news reporter on the campus newspaper news staff is the leading candidate for editor of the student newspaper next year. A student government cabinet member is a leading candidate for president of student government next year. One is male. One is female. They are currently dating. The student government leader is elected president. Should the relationship between the president-elect and the potential editor become a factor in considering her application for editor by a campus media committee? If she is not chosen, but remains on the staff, what type of assignments should she be given? If she is chosen editor, what can be done to avoid conflict of interest and retain the credibility of the news organization?

3. A student reporter for the campus television station is at the airport taking a friend to catch a flight back home. Coincidentally, the reporter sees the school's male baseball coach checking in at an airline counter with a female student known to the reporter. They appear to be going out of town for the weekend. The baseball coach is married. What should the reporter do? Investigate the story further? How would you handle this incident?

4. A staff photographer for the campus newspaper is out with friends for the evening at an off-campus nightclub. He never goes anywhere without his camera. At this club, the quarterback of the football team, an All-America and potential professional star, approaches another student at your school. Drunken shouting occurs, and punches are thrown. The photographer, motordrive whirring away, gets the action. The fight turns out to be over a female student. Are the photographs newsworthy? Why?

5. A student accidentally drowns in a campus swimming pool. A staff photographer for the campus television station happened to be nearby shooting another assignment. Frantic rescuers' efforts fail. A screaming roommate and an equally upset boyfriend are present to witness the entire event. The photographer has it all on tape, including closeups of the body being pulled from the pool and resting on the pool decking. As news director for the night's newscast, do you air the pictures with your story? If so, what pictures would you use? Which, if any, should not be used?

ASSIGNMENT 7.6

Write a code of ethics for your campus newspaper, magazine, radio station, or television station. Your code of ethics should be as specific as possible to situations on campus. You may want to use the codes in Appendices A, B, and C of the textbook as models.

ASSIGNMENT 7.7

To illustrate how local businesses and media advertising departments can put pressure on the newsroom, we will simulate a situation. Here are the players:

Setting: The newspaper is the *Everglades Citizen*, circulation 6,700 each Thursday. The community of Everglades, Fla., has a population of about 11,000 year-round residents. It is in rural east Collier County, near the Dade County border off the Tamiami Trail. The community is generally agricultural, but many residents make livings by guiding hunting and fishing tours of the Everglades and Big Cypress areas. The town has three grocery stores and two banks. There are two weekly newspapers, the *Citizen* and the new (two years old) *Everglades Sun*, also published on Thursdays, with a circulation of 5,500.

Publisher/Owner: He is Thomas McArthur, 37. He has run the *Everglades Citizen* for ten years. It is his newspaper company, owned entirely by the McArthur family. He also serves as advertising manager.

Publisher/Owner's Spouse: This is Wendy McArthur, 34. She is half owner, of course, and it is her parents' money that got the newspaper started a decade ago when the McArthurs bought a failing weekly for $20,000. She works part-time for the newspaper, mainly in display advertising production, but also helps with advertising sales when demand requires it.

Editor: This is Anna Hickcock, 26. She is a graduate of journalism program at the University of South Florida and has worked for the McArthurs for five years.

Reporter: Our enterprising reporter is Joan Dehli, 22. She is a recent graduate of the University of West Florida journalism program and this is her first job as a full-time reporter. She is one of two reporters on the staff of the newspaper. The other is a reporter-photographer.

Grocery Store Owner: She is Shirley Dickinson, 55, a resident of Marco Island. She owns a chain of four independent groceries (known, of course, as Dickinson's) in towns in west Collier County (in and around Naples and Fort Myers). One of her stores, the original store, is in Everglades. She is one of the leading advertisers in the newspaper on an annual ad lineage basis.

Grocery Store Manager: William Robert Stickney, 41, manages the Everglades store for Dickinson. Goes by "Billy Bob."

Customers/Readers: Most of the readers who shop at Dickinson's are long-time readers of the *Citizen*, but they are also often interested in the competition's new informative style. Some readers, of course, get the paper by home mail delivery on Fridays while others buy it in the grocery at the checkout counter.

THE SITUATION

Joan Dehli reads other newspapers around Florida. She is consumer-oriented and believes a "shopper's basket" story would benefit readers of her newspaper and would be a response to the aggressive style of the new *Sun*. So, on her own initiative, she calls the Department of Commerce in Washington and finds out what goes into a typical shopper's market basket according to federal government statisticians. With her list, she goes to each of the three grocery stores in town. She prices the items. She makes a list for each store by item and computes the cost of this grocery basket at each store.

While at Dickinson's, Manager Stickney notices her taking notes. He knows she is a reporter. He says nothing to her but tells Dickinson about it.

Dehli writes her story for next week's edition. Dickinson calls McArthur to ask what is going on. McArthur says he knows nothing. He asks his editor who asks Dehli.

Dehli shows both McArthur and Hickcock the story. Dickinson's looks bad, finishing a distant third in the cumulative price and in individual pricing of key food (e.g., milk, meat) items. McArthur calls Dickinson with the bad news.

What happens next? What do you do, Ms. Dickinson? As the grocery store owner and manager, what do you say to the publisher?

- As publisher, what do you think?
- What does the co-owner think?
- As publisher, what do you say to the editor?
- As editor, what do you say to the reporter?
- As reporter, what do you do?
- As readers, what can you do?
- As consumers, do you ever find out?

ASSIGNMENT 7.8

Discuss the following four situations in terms of how each should be covered in a news story. Your discussion should consider ethical standards in journalism, citing the codes of ethics in Appendices A, B, and C of the textbook.

1. A woman member of the County Commission is raped. The local newspaper reports she was hospitalized following an assault, but does not indicate it was a sexual attack. A conservative and anti-feminist, she has blocked the expenditure of public money for a rape crisis center at County Memorial Hospital. This has been a much-publicized local controversy for the past six months. But now she tells you that she plans to re-think her position on the crisis center. She also makes clear the deep personal trauma she is suffering as a result of the assault and asks that you not say she was raped in tomorrow morning's editions. What do you write? How do you handle the story?

2. The mayor is a hardliner on crime. He has made local drug enforcement a major issue. However, you learn that his 19-year-old son, who lives at home and attends a local community college, has been arrested for possession of a small quantity of marijuana. This is a misdemeanor if convicted. What do you do in handling this potential story? Would anything change if the illegal substance was cocaine?

3. A prominent local businessman identified with United Way and many other charitable causes is discovered to have embezzled $25,000 from one of the charities he heads. There is no question about his guilt, although charges have not yet been filed. The story, for the moment, is your newspaper's alone. When your reporter contacts this businessman for comment, the man says there are extenuating circumstances he cannot go into and that he will make full restitution if given a chance. He pleads that no story be written, saying his wife suffered a serious heart attack when news of this came to her. She is at an area hospital, and he fears that public disclosure of what he did will kill her. Do you run the story? What are your options?

4. A businessman donates $9.5 million to your university to build the long-awaited School of Communication Palace. As a campus newspaper reporter checking his background, you learn that the man was arrested at age 18 for armed robbery while a freshman at your school 40 years ago. He avoided serving time in prison by agreeing to enlist in the U.S. Army and by serving two years in Korea. His record, as far as you can tell, has been spotless since then. He refuses to talk about the incident, saying he has never even told his close friends or family about it. He seriously threatens to withdraw his contribution if the information is published in your newspaper or anywhere else. University officials are shocked when you reveal this information prior to publication to the vice president for Student Affairs, the School of Communication dean, and the university's Development Office staff. They say they knew nothing about it. Of course, they urge you to hold the story. Do you run the gift story, including information about the arrest? Do you take it to an off-campus publication not affiliated with your school? How do you handle it?

ASSIGNMENT 7.9

Write brief descriptions of your responses to the ethical situations posed below:

1. It's a big night at a nightclub near campus. Fraternities and sororities are celebrating, drinking a little, and having a good time. You assigned a photographer to take photos for a front page photograph. The photographer comes back with a group of fraternity brothers holding their beers high in the air and three of them offering a greeting in that familiar one finger salute. Do you run this photograph in the campus newspaper?

What do you say in the cutline?

Do you run this photograph in a neighborhood off-campus newspaper?

The regular main daily newspaper of your city?

2. The front-running candidate for mayor is holding a press conference. He is speaking comfortably and with ease. A reporter asks him about a political rival, a person who defeated him in a campaign for city commission three years ago. "Why, that little bastard. He's so full of shit, he's going to explode one day. I'm not going to meet him in a debate. I wouldn't give him a good kick in the ass," the candidate says with unexpected emotion. It is the best statement to come out of the event. Do you use the exact words in your news story? In print? On the air? Do you paraphrase?

3. You are the United Press International wire editor for your local newspaper. Along comes a story from Washington stating that a cabinet member (attorney general) of the United States government was overheard making a racist comment. The story contains the exact quote taken from an overheard conversation in a Washington hotel hallway. The individual says, "Those lazy drug-eating niggers are the biggest problem we have with crime in this town. Ship them back to where they came from and the problem would go away. I hate Washington these days. At least we got that goddamned mayor out of the way." Is this publishable in your newspaper? Can it be broadcast on a radio or television station? How do you handle it?

4. You have a photograph of a woman undergoing a breast cancer examination in a physician's office. She is nude from the waist up, but one of her breasts is blocked from view by the physician. Do you run this photograph with a story on the same subject?

5. You edit a monthly magazine inserted in the campus newspaper. One of your stories deals with unusual sexual behavior. In places, the story must get explicit to describe just how unusual this behavior can get. Some of the sources used in the story use rather direct, street-type language for these acts. The story is laced with common street terms. Do you use this type of language instead of a more clinical approach?

III | STYLE AND FORM

8 Newspaper and Magazine Writing Style

ASSIGNMENT 8.1

Correct these sentences for proper Associated Press and United Press International news writing style. Use your stylebook if necessary.

1. In his stress for unity, he said that "the flag is red, white, and blue, but we are the color of the rainbow, whites, blacks yellows.

2. He stressed that the democratic party cares and won't let the people of other nations down.

3. He referred to his "Rainbow Coalition", made up of the poor, minorities, small farmers and businessmen, as the "scapegoats of the values of corporate and economic policies" and called for the young to vote in great numbers, and for party policies to preserve the land and develop our resources.

4. "we must bring back stability", Reverend Jesse Jackson said, "we must fight for a change now".

5. "We must expand, heal, and unify our party," said Reverend Jackson, "We must seek a revival of spirit and share our burdens once again."

6. Leaders can change things . . . . . leadership can lead us to the promised land" Jackson said in trying to establish the goal of the Democratic party for the Presidential election, yesterday at the Democratic Convention in Atlanta, Georgia.

7. At the Democratic national Convention held in San Francisco, Friday July 13th, Jesse Jackson spoke out to a large group of supporters on the need for justice and equality for all people.

8. He called Mr. Reagans economic policies "voodoo economics," and he emphasized the fact that the two-hundred billion dollar deficit was more than the sum total of deficits of any previous administration.

9. According to the schedule in the press kit the bus was expected to leave for the convention hall at 9:00 o'clock in the morning.

10. Jackson called for a meeting of the black congressional caucus immediately after the convention session that morning in the Magnolia Ballroom of the Peachbasket Hotel at 11:45.

11. The report stated that Jesse Jackson has sold his 23% share of stock in the company.

12. "Lackey! Get me a coke!" he shouted. "But do it after you make those xerox copies of the new band-aid designs."

ASSIGNMENT 8.2

Contact your local newspaper or a local magazine office to ask whether the newspaper or magazine has a stylebook. Does it use a wire service stylebook or has it developed one of its own? How is the stylebook localized for particular usages unique to your own community?

ASSIGNMENT 8.3

Can you find examples of sexism in writing in newspapers and magazines you read? How do these examples violate the principles set forth in *The Washington Post*'s guidelines on sexism in writing? (See Chapter 8 of the textbook.)

ASSIGNMENT 8.4

As a team project, prepare a campus stylebook supplement for your class. This stylebook should include such things as correct names of buildings, streets, academic titles, and so forth.

ASSIGNMENT 8.5

Read your campus newspaper's most recent issue for style usage problems. How could the writing and meaning be improved if writers had followed a stylebook a bit more closely? Can you find examples of style rules being broken on a regular basis?

ASSIGNMENT 8.6

Abbreviations

Find the style errors in these sentences and make the necessary corrections. Some sentences may be correct.

1. "Governor Martinez promised he would read the legislation by tomorrow," said the mayor.
2. His company wanted to remove any remaining chemicals from the Lewis Corporation dump site.
3. The report came from the Occupational Safety and Health Administration (OSHA).
4. Kennedy represents the State of Massachusetts.
5. The flood killed scores of people in Corpus Christi, Tex.

ASSIGNMENT 8.7

Numerals

Find the style errors in these sentences and make the necessary corrections. Some sentences may be correct.

1. The six-year-old boy was abandoned by his father.
2. The 10th Amendment addresses the rights of states.
3. Most baby boomers were born in the Fifties.
4. The weather forecaster predicted winds of five to 10 miles per hour.
5. The model wore a size five dress.

ASSIGNMENT 8.8

Capitalization

Find the style errors in these sentences and make the necessary corrections. Some sentences may be correct.

1. She first ordered a Manhattan Cocktail.
2. They gave the award to Journalism Professor Carol J. Brooks.
3. The History Department has the highest number of undergraduates.
4. The setting of the play was Rome, 96 A.D.
5. The Black population of Detroit is larger than Cleveland's.

ASSIGNMENT 8.9

Times and dates

Find the style errors in these sentences and make the necessary corrections. Some sentences may be correct.

1. The event begins at 4 p.m. this afternoon.
2. He will begin the job next Tuesday.
3. The firefighters rescued Tuesday six children from the burning house.
4. The appointment was for 9:00 a.m.
5. The hostages were to be released at 3 p.m.–9 a.m. EDT.

ASSIGNMENT 8.10

Titles

Find the style errors in these sentences and make the necessary corrections. Some sentences may be correct.

1. The president's wife, Mrs. Barbara Bush, invited the governor's wife to the White House.
2. The Rev. Jesse Jackson has run twice for the presidency.
3. The President met with the Pope on Friday.
4. Dead Poet's Society remains a popular movie.
5. "Gone with the Wind" takes place during the Civil War.

ASSIGNMENT 8.11

Punctuation

Find the style errors in these sentences and make the necessary corrections. Some sentences may be correct.

1. ". . . I have always tried to do what was best for this university," . . . the provost said.
2. She will visit Gary, Ind. before she goes to Hacienda Heights, Calif.
3. They were getting ready for the three-day weekend festivities.
4. In the '50s, she brought home A's and B's.
5. He appeared deus ex machina to save the farmer's daughter from the villain.

ASSIGNMENT 8.12

Addresses

Find the style errors in these sentences and make the necessary corrections. Some sentences may be correct.

1. The incident occurred at Seven August Rd.
2. The reception begins at 6 p.m. Friday, 1600 Joseph Blake Dr.
3. Meet us at Honig and Radcliffe Avenues.
4. John Jones of 9107 Riggs Lane was arrested yesterday.
5. The abandoned house, 704 East 51st St., once had been a mansion.

ASSIGNMENT 8.13

Sexism

Find the style errors in these sentences and make the necessary corrections. Some sentences may be correct.

1. Marvin Jones was named chairperson of the bar association's minority affairs committee.
2. His fiancee was a curvaceous blond bombshell.
3. Joan Gray, the new mayor, has five children in elementary school.
4. Barbara Jordan was a congressman from Texas.
5. She had always wanted to be a fireman.

ASSIGNMENT 8.14

Miscellaneous

Find the style errors in these sentences and make the necessary corrections. Some sentences may be correct.

1. He's no different than your father.
2. Give me your book which is on the table.
3. The pilot said that he had flown a 747 before.
4. The refugees escaped to freedom in the west.
5. They ordered that he be executed to death.
6. The youth was sent to prison for his part in the purse snatching.
7. There were several persons waiting for the parade to begin.
8. The federally-funded program will end at the beginning of October.
9. Alaniz was imprisoned in February, 1988, after being accused of killing her husband.
10. The 18th state ranked team will play their home games on Ralph Miller Court.

9 Broadcast Writing Style

Your radio station's assignment editor has given you the higher education beat. As the writer on that beat, you have to rewrite a press release from the University of Miami that came in the mail this afternoon.

Your assignment editor needs a story that will run 0:45. It must be exactly that length—no more, no less. Time your script and write the time at the bottom of the last page.

Write and rewrite as necessary. It is your script. Type a clean (and neat) script as well. More errors in your typing and editing means more mistakes when the story is read on the air.

There is no need for introductions or other material. The anchors for our all-news station will take care of that for us. Our station serves the Miami-Fort Lauderdale market.

Remember to follow your broadcast news style book in preparing the manuscript.

Office of Public Affairs
P.O. Box 248105
Coral Gables, FL 33124
(305) 284-5500

Contact: Conchita Ruiz-Topinka
Date: July 30, 1990

N E W S

AT&T CHAIRMAN TO SPEAK IN MIAMI ON AUGUST 9

CORAL GABLES--Robert Allen, chairman and chief executive officer of AT&T, will speak on the global promise of the information age at 11:30 a.m. on Thursday, August 9, at the Miami Airport Hilton Hotel.

Part of the University of Miami School of Business Administration Corporate Affiliate Program, the talk is titled, "Internationally Speaking: Why the Global Promise of the Information Age Won't Wait." Allen will examine how information technology has become the lifeblood of international business and a source of competitive advantage for companies with vision.

AT&T, a leader in information technology development, has expanded from a primary telecommunications oriented company to the much broader business of information movement and management. It supports businesses around the world with advanced telecommunication services.

Allen was elected chairman and CEO of AT&T in April 1988. He began his career at Indiana Bell in 1957. Subsequently, he served in officer posts there and at Bell of Pennsylvania, Illinois Bell, the Chesapeake and Potomac Telephone Companies, and AT&T. He was named president and chief operating officer of AT&T in 1986.

His corporate board memberships include Bristol-Myers Company, Manufacturers Hanover Corporation and the Manufacturers Hanover Trust Company.

The Miami Airport Hilton Hotel is located at 5101 Blue Lagoon Drive, off S.R. 836 (Dolphin Expressway) at the Red Road exit. The cost for the luncheon is $20 per person. Reservations may be made by calling (305) 284-4643.

-30-

ASSIGNMENT 9.2

Part of using radio well includes permitting the public to hear for itself. That means using the sounds and voices rather than just the announcer's description. Good editing can shorten an interview and, in the end, enhance it. To do this, you must integrate the tape into the script, which then sets up the soundbite with identification from the speaker but does not give away the substance of the "quote."

You can use any of the interview transcript below for your story. Assume you have tape. Do not forget incues and outcues, of course.

From the following transcript of an interview, write three radio "packages" for use this morning on the air. Two should be 45 seconds long, and the other should be 1:15. You choose. For ease in timing, use your watch. You must not go over or under the time permitted. Be exact.

The Situation

You have just taped an interview with Mayor Anthony Thomas following a news conference in which he announced severe budget cuts for city services. Total reductions in the $146,000,000 budget amount to $13,450,000. The police department will lose 12% of its patrol force and special units for juveniles and sex crimes. The fire department will close one station on the far east side at NW 72nd Street and Alameda Avenue and will trim one man from its three-men-per-truck teams. Rumors of cuts have been going around for days, and a group of east side residents has filed a petition asking for a grand jury investigation of city finances.

The Interview Transcript

You: What's the cause of this 15% cut in the budget?

Thomas: Well . . . it's not really 15%, more like 9 or 10.

You: Whatever it is, what is the problem?

Thomas: Not enough money coming in.

You: From where?

Thomas: The usual sources of city revenue: utility charges and sales taxes . . . the hotel-motel tax is way down, too, but the city doesn't get that money directly for government expenses. It goes to arts and tourist promotion and things like that. I guess it's just the economy in general, and, of course, we won't be getting any more of that good federal matching money which was at least 10 or 11 million last year.

You: Couldn't city officials see that coming?

Thomas: Apparently not.

You: How badly will this hurt the citizens?

Thomas: Well . . . they aren't going to like having fewer cops on the street, and I don't know what will happen to the crime rate. That always gets people upset. The fire department is in trouble, too, but Chief Davis tells me his people will just do the best they can.

You: Speaking of the fire department, why was the decision made to cut station 6 on Alameda after all the fight about getting one out there a few years ago? Surely someone expected the east-siders to get mad about that.

Thomas: Someone always gets mad. The department said that one makes the fewest runs, so it seemed all right to me.

You: But statistics used at the time of the fight showed that the dollar loss per fire out there was greater than any other fires because of the long response time.

Thomas: Maybe the chief thought better a few big fires than a lot of small ones.

You: I don't understand.

Thomas: I mean . . . maybe it's better to have bigger loss in a few fires than to have a bunch of small ones that get bigger . . . or something like that. Ask Davis, that's his thing.

You: You didn't say anything at the press conference about new taxes or other ways to raise money.

Thomas: Well . . . of course we will study the problem. Of course, if business is down, then sales taxes are going to stay down, unless we raise the rate of tax, and I don't think people would be too crazy about that. The state can't help and the feds can't help. Maybe the best thing would be a group of citizens to come up with a proposal or proposals that could provide some money.

You: I didn't notice anything in your statement about cutting some other city services like garbage collection or going up on the rates for water and sewer. Have you considered these?

Thomas: I'm sure the commission members and the city staff have looked at these options and just didn't think that was the way to solve the problem.

You: Won't this appear to be what some people have already called a plan to scare folks into voting for more taxes because they're worried about fire and police protection, when it could be solved in another way?

Thomas: I don't care what some people think. They're not doing anything to solve the problem. We're doing the best we can.

You: People on the east side don't think so, apparently. Does the grand jury petition bother you? Is there any basis for the complaints?

Thomas: The east side always complains. They complain about everything we do for them. All they're doing is getting in the way.

You: When will this emergency be over?

Thomas: I guess when people realize we need more money . . . maybe taxes, maybe less service, maybe some bright idea. It could go on a long time.

You: Thank you, Mayor Thomas.

Thomas: Thank you.

ASSIGNMENT 9.3

The following press releases came into the newsroom in today's mail. You are assigned to write either one story of 1:15 or two separate stories totaling 1:15 for the 6 p.m. newscast today for your favorite local radio station. Assume the information is current. Be sure to indicate the name of the station for your instructor's benefit. And be sure to consider the audience of your station as you prepare your script(s).

Time your script length. List the time for each story. You must be exact. Put the time at the top of the script. Since you cannot use all the information that is provided, use only what is necessary.

April 12, 1990
NOTE TO CORRESPONDENTS—UNITED STATES POPULATION ESTIMATES, BY AGE,
SEX, RACE, AND HISPANIC ORIGIN: 1989

For more information contact Public Information Office (301) 763–4040.
For Release Wed., April 11, 1990
CB90–68

A report containing estimates of the U.S. population for 1989 by single years of age to 100, sex, race, and Hispanic origin has been published by the Commerce Department's Census Bureau.

A similar report for 1988 was released on March 2, 1990 (CB90–38), Series P–25, No. 1045. The 1988 report includes a more detailed analysis of population trends, methods, and sources of data.

The 1989 report includes estimates for 1986 to 1989, covering the total population including armed forces overseas, the resident population, and the civilian population.

Race categories for which age-sex distributions are shown include White, Black, and Other Races. Estimates of the resident population by sex also are presented for the Asian or Pacific Islander, and the American Indian, Eskimo, or Aleut populations.

The report includes an analysis of year-to-year changes in the total population from 1980 through 1989 and the major components of births, deaths, and net civilian immigration.

Copies of the report, "United States Population Estimates, by Age, Sex, Race, and Hispanic Origin: 1989," Series P–25, No. 1957, are available prepaid from the Superintendent of Documents, U.S. Government Printing Office, Washington, D.C. 20402.

Change in Population, by Age Group, Sex, Race, and Hispanic Origin: July 1, 1980 to July 1, 1989

(Numbers in thousands. Includes Armed Forces overseas.)

Subject	Population on July 1 1989	Population on July 1 1980	Population change, 1980–89 Number	Population change, 1980–89 Percent	Average annual percent change
Total, all ages..........	248,762	227,767	21,006	9.2	1.0
Under 5 years	18,752	16,453	2,295	13.9	1.5
5 to 13 years	31,834	31,095	733	2.4	0.3
14 to 17 years..........	13,486	16,142	(2,646)	−16.4	−2.0
18 to 24 years..........	26,564	30,360	(3,785)	−12.5	1.5
25 to 34 years..........	44,048	37,625	6,423	17.1	1.8
35 to 44 years..........	36,584	25,868	10,716	41.4	3.9
45 to 54 years..........	24,905	22,754	2,151	9.5	1.0
55 to 64 years..........	21,593	21,762	(168)	− 0.8	−0.1
65 to 74 years..........	18,182	15,653	2,529	16.2	1.7
77 to 84 years..........	9,761	7,781	1,979	25.4	2.5
85 years, over..........	3,042	2,269	772	34.0	3.3
65 years, over..........	30,984	25,704	5,280	20.5	2.1
Male	121,445	110,888	10,557	9.5	1.0
Female..................	127,317	116,869	10,448	8.9	1.0
White	209,326	195,571	13,755	7.0	0.8
Black....................	30,788	26,903	3,885	14.4	1.5
Other races.............	8,647	5,283	3,365	63.7	5.5
Asian or Pacific Islander (1)	6,881	3,834	3,047	78.5	6.5
American Indian, Eskimo, or Aleut (1)	1,737	1,429	308	21.6	2.2
Hispanic origin (2).............	20,528	14,803	5,724	38.7	3.6

(1) Resident population

(2) Persons of Hispanic origin may be of any race.

April 3, 1990
THERE'S STILL TIME TO RETURN YOUR 1990 CENSUS
QUESTIONNAIRE

For more information contact Public Information Office (301) 763–4040. For Immediate Release CB90–N90.05

If you haven't yet mailed back your completed 1990 census questionnaire, there's still time to do so.

"Though April 1 was officially Census Day," explains Census Bureau Director Barbara Everitt Bryant, "we can still accept completed questionnaires a week or so after April 1 because our computers will be able to log them in before we create the list of households not returning the form.

Over 88 million census forms were mailed to households on March 23 and another 11 million were delivered directly to households by census personnel for mailing back. All census questionnaire packages contain an instruction guide and a postage paid return envelope.

Anyone needing assistance completing their form may call the following toll-free numbers and receive help in their native language.

English:	1–800–999–1990	Spanish:	1–800–283–6826
Chinese:	1–800–365–2101	Korean:	1–800–444–6205
Laotian:	1–800–888–3208	Vietnamese:	1–800–937–1953
Thai:	1–800–288–1984		

The hearing impaired may call 1–800–777–0978 for TDD assistance.

Starting in late April, an army of follow-up census takers will visit those households that haven't yet returned their questionnaire.

"Being included in the census is important to your community because census results are used to divide political power and to allocate billions of dollars in federal funds each year," Bryant said.

Reprinted with the permission of the Department of Commerce, Bureau of the Census.

ASSIGNMENT 9.4

Writing for the ear is a challenge. Writing for the eye and ear is a doubly difficult broadcast news writing task for the neophyte television writer. This type of writing demands that you not only write for detail and factual accuracy, but that you also concern yourself with writing for the ear in a manner that is conversational yet precise.

Writing a script for a 1:30 to 1:45 television news package is not a quick job. You must consider the sound of your story, that is, what you have to say and how it sounds to listeners/viewers. But you must also write for the eye because of the visual element of your story. Finally, keep in mind that your audience may be offended by some of the content of your interview. What should you use? Omit?

The Assignment

You must write a 1:40 package for today's newscast. It goes on the air at 6 p.m. The script must be in your executive producer's hands on time or you are penalized. Don't be late! Write your script with attention to the visual elements of the story today. For practical purposes in lab, consider that you have the pictures you need (but describe them briefly). Visuals include such things as videotape shot on location, file tape as needed, slides made from still photographs, character-generated images for the screen, graphics, and so on.

The Situation

The Knights of the Ku Klux Klan plan to produce a television program, *Florida Klan News*, which will be aired in about two weeks. The show would open with a burning cross. It will be a half hour each time it is aired, and it will be shown on cable television only.

Because of federal access laws in broadcasting, there is little owners of cable franchises can do. The first program will be aired in Altamonte Springs, about 17 miles from Disney World in Central Florida. The cable franchise operator is Storer Cable Communications.

Other cities have tried to stop cable programming and have failed in the courts. Miami is one of them. New York and Kansas City have also tried to restrict what is shown on cable. Miami tried to stop what some called pornographic programming. Kansas City officials are trying to keep a KKK show off the air and are currently in court. In the past, courts have ruled that the First Amendment protections of freedom of speech apply to local cable access channels and community programming.

Our Chopper 13 pilot flies you to talk to the main source. You interviewed the Grand Wizard of the KKK, Joe Bob Lovett of Apopka, Florida. You need to get this story on the air tonight. The tape you shot is at Lovett's home in a den, with the two of you sitting on a sofa.

The Interview

You: Are you planning to go on the air soon?

Lovett: Yes, in about two weeks if things go right.

You: What is the show like?

Lovett: It will be a little bit radical.

You: What do you mean?

Lovett: You'll see. Watch it. We'll open with our traditional burning cross.

You: How many people will watch it?

Lovett: I don't know for sure, but I do know there are 16,000 households connected to the cable system at this time.

You: There are many people who do not like your group. Can Storer do anything to refuse to run the program?

Lovett: The only way they can keep it off is if the tape is poor quality or because I am cussing or use profanity. I'm not ignorant or stupid. It will be very, very professional, and they cannot use that reason to stop from putting our program on the air.

You: Are there other regulations?

Lovett: I'm paying a fee . . . a $200 fee. I'm paying for my time. There is nothing they can do about it.

You: Many experts think this freedom of access means cable is like an electronic soap box. You can stand up in the park, in this case, the cable studio, and say what you want. Is that what you are doing?

Lovett: It is. In fact, as long as it is not obscene, indecent, or inflammatory, there is little many authorities or other people can do about it. And this is what Storer's own attorneys have told me.

You: How long did it take to make your first program?

Lovett: About two and a half hours.

You: Is it now finished?

Lovett: Yes. I am taking it to Storer on Monday.

You: Describe the program in more detail. What will viewers see?

Lovett: After we open with the cross burning at night, the tape shows me in a business suit talking with other members of Ku Klux Chapter 87. I then begin talking with Chapter Grand Dragon Bill Johnson who is wearing his $150 white silk hooded robe with five stripes on the sleeve that indicate his rank.

You: Why are you wearing a suit? Why not your own robe?

Lovett: I am a candidate for sheriff of Lake County. I did it for image reasons . . . It's purely political, you know.

You: What else does the tape show?

Lovett: We have some tape of recent Klan rallies, then we present some information about upcoming events, some letters for . . . and against . . . the group. We then provide some recommended conservative reading materials and finish with a call for new membership and contributions.

You: Do you have any more programs in progress?

Lovett: Nothing is on tape yet. We do have outlines for future programs. We plan to interview Jewish rabbis, prostitutes, and crack dealers. It will be open format . . . nothing derogatory, no profanity, but a little bit racial.

You: The Klan has always been strong in its language about other groups. How will you refer to Blacks, Hispanics, Jews, and others?

Lovett: We will be specific in our references to other ethnic and racial groups. We believe these groups should be called by their historical and traditional names. We will call niggers 'niggers' or 'spooks', we will call poor whites 'crackers', and we will be straight forward. We don't believe in glossing over things.

You: What else do you plan to say?

Lovett: We will certainly have a message of preservation of the Anglo-Saxon ideas, culture, and all the fruits thereof.

You: Who will watch this show?

Lovett: The niggers and Jew-boys will. We think members of racial and religious minority groups will watch us just to see what we are doing. They are a little intimidated by us. They will watch to know what we are doing and not be running around in front of your house. We want the program to be a way to rally to control the influx of nonwhites into this country, to prevent foreign people from buying up all our property, to limit imports, and to become more involved in catching criminals.

You: How will you raise money to keep this program on the air?

Lovett: We will sell Klan T-shirts, caps and visors, and bumper stickers to raise money. We will also seek donations.

You: Will this program, if successful, be expanded?

Lovett: You bet your . . . oops, guess I'd better be careful. This is television isn't it? Let me start over . . . Yes. I'd like to see it on cable systems in Orlando and Tampa and Jacksonville. We have studio and production time donated by a member, so that helps cut costs now.

You: And not in Miami?

Lovett: No, too many niggers, spics and Jews . . . err . . . make that Blacks, Hispanics, and Jews . . . live there and run the cable systems. We want to start where our message will be respected and where it will get a positive response. We think Central Floridians understand us better. There's just too many foreigners in Miami. That town's not even American any more. The real Americans are all moving to Orlando and Tampa.

You: Uh . . . uh . . . want to say anything else?

Lovett: No. Thanks for coming here.

You: Thank you Mr. Lovett.

ASSIGNMENT 9.5

Telephone the news director at a local television or radio station. Ask him or her if you can have a copy of a recent newscast script. Look it over for form and style. How are corrections and other changes in the script made?

ASSIGNMENT 9.6

Take a newspaper article and convert it to a radio news script. How much reorganization and revision are necessary? Why?

ASSIGNMENT 9.7

Tape record a local radio or television newscast. Then type a transcript for one of the packages you taped and analyze how the story was prepared and aired.

ASSIGNMENT 9.8

Contact the nearest Associated Press or United Press International bureau or a local radio station to ask for hard copy from its broadcast wire service machines. Read through these stories for style and usage. Do you see any problems in the stories? Are they easy to read aloud? Why or why not?

ASSIGNMENT 9.9

With your instructor's assistance, invite a local broadcast journalist to your class to discuss how he or she prepared a recent story from beginning to end. Ask your guest to focus on writing and script preparation.

10 | Quotations, Soundbites, Attribution, IDs

ASSIGNMENT 10.1

Contact a local broadcast or print journalist and prepare a memorandum or report that runs three to five pages on that person's interviewing style and general approach to interviewing.

In this report, you will be certain to include the following information:

1. A brief biographical sketch of this person.

2. The actual job assignment and responsibilities and their relationship to interviewing approaches.

3. Ideas about interviewing as a reporting tool.

4. To what extent does this person do background work on interviews?

5. How does this person develop rapport with the source?

6. Are there any distinctive interviewing/questioning techniques this person uses?

7. How does the interview fit into the general pattern of the person's work? Is it central? Peripheral?

8. How does this person's approach to interviewing compare with that of others in the business?

ASSIGNMENT 10.2

For today, you will write a story about someone else in class. Pair up and start asking questions.

In your interview-based story, try to find out something interesting and unusual about the person you have selected. Devise questions to find out biographical background, personal interests, academic goals, professional career goals, and even an embarrassing anecdote or two to brighten up the story.

Your story should have plenty of direct quotations in it. Make this person come alive through his or her own words. Try to include some descriptive passages.

You are writing this story for your campus newspaper's life-styles or features section.

ASSIGNMENT 10.3

Melissa Wright, the reporter, is 25 years old and works for the *Sunniland Times*. She wants to interview the head of the County Welfare Department concerning custody of triplets—babies born prematurely to poor parents six weeks ago. Publicity of the case had angered the conservative community, and all groups involved in keeping the babies from their parents—the courts, the hospital administration, the doctors, the county welfare people—have come under attack. The head of the welfare board does not want to talk about the case with anyone, especially not a representative of the newspaper which first reported the case. Final custody of the children is still undecided. The reporter must convince the head of the Department of Welfare to agree to an interview. She has arrived at the office at 3 p.m. and finds the secretary absent from her desk. She speaks to the head of the welfare board directly as he comes out of his office for coffee.

The head of the welfare board is John Murray, 44 years old and highly intelligent. He belongs to many organizations, including the Democratic Party, the Catholic Church, and even the National Organization for Women (NOW). He is used to being in charge. He grew up in Los Angeles and moved to Sunniland after receiving a B.A. in social work from the University of Wisconsin at Madison in 1972. He earned an M.S. in social work from Yale in 1974. He is married but has no children. The controversy created over the triplets case as reported in *The Times* has angered Murray and made him resentful toward the news media. He tends to be serious and moody, but he is open minded and listens to arguments—except on the subject of the triplets. As a welfare administrator, he usually believes that children should remain with their parents if possible. He perceives the interviewer, Melissa, as a young, aggressive journalist who wants this story for a promotion. He thinks she would say and do anything to get this story. He does not trust her. Murray is convinced he should not be interviewed, especially on the record, since his superiors downtown are watching over his shoulder on this one. He is also up for a promotion.

The assignment: Convince Murray to agree to the interview.

What do you say to him?

ASSIGNMENT 10.4

Here's a recently published story that was based on a telephone interview. Was the story limited in any way because of the telephone? Would an in-person interview have made the story better? Why? Finally, would you have used the seven "dirty" words if this had been your story?

NEWSPAPER: *The Miami Herald*
DATE: Friday, May 29, 1987
AUTHOR/REPORTER: Linda R. Thornton
TITLE: Arts Writer
HEADLINE: FCC rule no joke to Carlin
PAGE: 1D

First there were seven—"dirty" words, that is—words that the Federal Communications Commission banned from radio or TV.

Those seven no-nos weren't determined by a panel of language experts or a public opinion poll but were taken from a satirical monologue recorded in 1973 by comedian George Carlin, who will appear at Sunrise Musical Theater Saturday.

Last month, the FCC announced an even stricter policy toward obscene and indecent language on the air. The commission warned that it would penalize broadcasters and stations that air not only the forbidden seven, but also any others that describe "sexual or excretory activities or organs."

One might imagine that this shift of attention away from the Carlin list would cause the 50-year-old comic some relief.

But Carlin, who started his career as a disc jockey, says he's deeply concerned about the FCC's latest move.

"These people are political appointees who are advancing the Republican right-wing agenda. They've been frustrated at everything else they've tried, so now this is something they can do without going through Congress," said Carlin in a telephone interview this week.

"What these people don't seem to recognize is that there are two knobs on the radio that represent freedom of choice, which is what the United States is based on, in a loose sense. These two knobs—one of them turns it off; the other one changes the station. But these organized morality vigilantes are the ones who are responsible for most of the problem."

Carlin has always had a special fondness for, and way with, words. The ironies and absurdities behind everyday language have made up much of his material since he began to shift away from drug-related and political humor in the late '70s. One example is the "Love and Regards" bit on his latest album, *Playin' With Your Head:* "They'll say, 'Tell Klaus Rebecca sends her love!' Suppose you don't see Klaus? What do you do with her love, carry it around?"

A long-time supporter of freedom of choice and speech, Carlin has used racy language in his act since the early 1970s, when he was fired from a Las Vegas hotel for saying "s——" on stage and later arrested for using profanity during a performance in Milwaukee.

But it was his now famous "Seven Dirty Words" routine played on the radio that brought him to infamy when an irate parent's complaint led to the FCC ban in 1978. This policy and the general restrictiveness of most of network television turned Carlin toward the freedom of cable TV. Every year or two, he appears in an HBO special (another is scheduled for release next spring).

Now touring on weekends only, Carlin is directing much of his attention towards films. He appeared in a supporting role as a burned-out aging hippie in the recent film *Outrageous Fortune* and just completed another, *Bill and Ted's Excellent Adventure,* in which he plays, "Rufus, a cool guy from the future."

Throughout most of the '70s, Carlin's humor focused on drugs, politics and the environment—popular topics then with young counter-culture audiences. But as he and his fans grew older, Carlin began to revamp his style toward more universal topics, such as losing things ("The first thing that happens when you get to heaven is you get back everything you ever lost . . . you get back all your wallets . . . no cash, though—it's just like Earth") or ways to keep people alert ("Go into a photography studio and ask to buy pictures of other people—how much for that heavyset couple in the window?")

In his show at Sunrise Saturday, audiences can expect to hear more Carlinesque word play, including new routines on oxymorons and redundancies. And he'll probably end the show with his trademark dirty words list, expanded over the years to more than 400 "impolite" words which he rattles off like an auctioneer.

"I have shown all these years that I can be funny with or without words like that, but . . . I like the feeling of yes or no, I can use them or not," he said. "I think it adds a certain amount of spice and emphasis to certain types of characters that I might be doing or to certain passages where I'm expressing my own thoughts. It gives me the full range of expression that's open to most adult humans—and a lot of younger ones, too."

Reprinted with the permission of *The Miami Herald.*

ASSIGNMENT 10.5

Following are two U.S. Department of Commerce press releases from the Bureau of the Census public relations office that are typical of releases that arrive in the newsroom mail on a daily basis. These releases would rarely be used without revision or rewriting, even in the smallest publications. Nor would these be broadcast without significant changes. Releases such as these are too laden with bureaucrat-ese to make for good reading or listening. Yet, the Census Bureau has designed these for information for the public and for the news media.

Most news organizations, if interested in this information for a story, would probably assign a reporter to handle the story, and the reporter would use the release as a starting point to develop his or her own story.

Take a look at these two releases and think about how you would handle these if you were assigned to write stories from them. Write a 500-word summary about how you would develop stories from these releases and from what *local* sources you would seek quotations and/or soundbites.

POPULATION PROFILE OF THE UNITED STATES: 1989

For more information contact Public Information Office (301) 763–4040
For Release Friday, June 9, 1989
CB89–96
WASHINGTON, D.C.—A new U.S. population profile has been issued by
the Commerce Department's Census Bureau. The profile, drawn primarily from
bureau reports published in 1988, is illustrated by color charts and graphs.

Subjects include national and state population trends and projections, metropolitan and nonmetropolitan populations, city and suburban populations, farm
population, migration, school enrollment, educational attainment, household and
families, marital status and living arrangements, and fertility.

The profile also contains data on the labor force, occupations, family money
income, and poverty.

Sections not previously included in the profile cover the Black, Hispanic, and
elderly populations.

Copies of the report, "Population Profile of the United States: 1989," Series
P–23, No. 159, are available prepaid from the Superintendent of Documents,
U.S. Government Printing Office, Washington, D.C. 20402. (Source: Compu-
Serve, June 12, 1989).

Reprinted with the permission of the Department of Commerce, Bureau of the Census.

HISPANICS HAVE HIGHER RATES OF MOVING
THAN OTHER GROUPS, CENSUS BUREAU REPORTS

For more information contact Public Information Office, (301) 763–4040
For Release Thursday, May 11, 1989
CB89–SP.03

WASHINGTON, D.C.—Hispanics had higher rates of moving than non-Hispanic Whites or Blacks from March 1986 to March 1987, according to the Commerce Department's Census Bureau.

Twenty-three percent of the nation's 18.4 million Hispanics (age one year and older) moved from one residence to another in that period.

The rates were 17 percent for non-Hispanic Whites and 20 percent for Blacks.

Hispanics had the highest rate of local movement; 18 percent moved within the same county compared with 14 percent for Blacks and 11 percent for non-Hispanic Whites.

Hispanics also had a higher rate of movement from abroad (2 percent), and lower rates of movement within states (3 percent) and between states (2 percent) than non-Hispanic Whites.

Copies of the report, "Geographic Mobility: March 1986 to March 1987," Series P–20, No. 430, are available prepaid from the Superintendent of Documents, U.S. Government Printing Office, Washington, D.C. 20402.

Reprinted with the permission of the Department of Commerce, Bureau of the Census.

ASSIGNMENT 10.6

Set up a class debate on the merits of altering quotations. You will probably find some classmates who oppose changing quotations or selectively editing soundbites and actualities for cosmetic reasons. Others may feel minor changes are acceptable. Discuss the merits of each position. Discuss whether dialect is appropriate. How do you feel about the matter? If a debate is not possible, write a 500-word position paper on this issue.

ASSIGNMENT 10.7

Can you find any recent examples of offensive language in a news story in print or on the air? When is it appropriate to use offensive language in a direct quotation, a soundbite, or an actuality? Are there any circumstances? Write a 500-word essay on circumstances affecting use of offensive language in news writing. Be sure to consider your community's *local standards*.

ASSIGNMENT 10.8

Create a list of offensive or "red-flag" words which might lead to trouble if published or broadcast in your community or on your campus—even if they are exact words from a source. Is there a difference in community standards and campus standards? Why?

ASSIGNMENT 10.9

Look for examples of news stories in which sources of information have been poorly attributed or not attributed at all. How could these problems have been remedied?

ASSIGNMENT 10.10

News stories with anonymous sources are often troublesome to audiences. Can you find recent examples of news stories that used an anonymous source or did not completely identify a source? Is the usage appropriate? Write a 500-word essay to analyze your example.

ASSIGNMENT 10.11

Look at the following direct and indirect quotations and correct punctuation and quotation marks. (Do not insert quotation marks unless they are already part of the sentence. Assume such sentences are indirect quotes.)

1. "When the building was originally built in 1967 that option was provided for", Kratzer said.

2. "The part disrupted will be the entry from the North lawn." Kratzer said. "we'll take a piece of railing off the second floor walkway and build stairs next to the Union."

3. Kratzer said, the project will be done in 300 days.

4. "If things go right" he said, "We could have it done by next Homecoming.

5. Neely said "things will have started to slow down on campus by that time."

6. The walkway on the Union's north side will be covered Kratzer said.

7. The second round of bids brought the desired price, "But the lowest bidder couldn't be used," Neely said.

8. The conference room, said Neely will be used by the Student Senate, among others.

9. He said The stairs will extend two flights instead of three.

10. When the expansion is created, Neely said the Union will have 15 more meeting rooms that can house about 350 people, and a lecture hall that can seat about 130 people.

ASSIGNMENT 10.12

In the following exercises you are provided background information and quotes. Write the story.

Item 1:

(From *The Independent Alligator,* University of Florida):

A free rape-prevention and self-defense seminar will be held at noon on Saturday. The seminar, which will last four hours, will demonstrate how rape can be prevented. Other topics include what a woman can do if she is attacked and where she can go for help if she does become a rape victim. You get this information from Dan Loman, manager at Y.K. Kim's Tae Kwon Do and Nautilus, which will host the event at 400 Newberry Road in Gainesville. Here is what you have in direct quotes from Loman:

"The rape problem is really bad in Gainesville. Maybe we can stop some of the terrible things that are happening."

Loman also tells you that Maggie Gerard, a counselor with the Rape Victim Advocate Program, will discuss the services the program provides for victims of rape. In 1989, the program helped 245 victims through personal and legal problems. The Gainesville Police Department's Officer Friendly Program, Alpine Boarding Kennels and Crime Prevention Security Systems also will make presentations.

Tae Kwon Do instructors Dean Hazard and David Donahue will demonstrate techniques women can use to escape from attackers.

Here's a direct quote from Donahue, a fourth-degree black belt and instructor for 14 years:

"These methods are simple and effective. You don't have to be a black belt to make them work."

Item 2:

(From *The Independent Alligator,* University of Florida):

Monday afternoon 14 board members of the Community Council on Alcohol and Drug Abuse gave unanimous support of a state bill calling for a 2 percent tax on the distribution of beer in Florida. The council has 23 board members from different parts of the community.

The volunteer organization was founded in 1983 to increase awareness of substance abuse rather than end it, said CCADA president Patti Greenough. There are 400 members in the organization.

CCADA holds monthly forums, participates in "Just Say No" contests in elementary schools, prints informational brochures and sponsors workshops on substance abuse.

The bill was debated during the last legislative session but was not passed. It will be reintroduced to the Florida legislature Jan. 31.

Sam Clark is one of the board members. He said the tax would generate an estimated $65 million annually for alcohol and drug treatment and rehabilitation.

Here's a direct quote from Clark: "People will be taking out an insurance policy for their future."

Here's exactly what Greenough said: "We see ourselves as a piece of the pie, and people must get involved in their own areas in order to have a drug-free community. Our main objective is to get people aware of the council and what we have to offer the community."

University of Florida Student Affairs Vice President Art Sandeen serves on the council. He said the group (and here's his quote) "raises awareness and makes community members knowledgeable to the commitment to fight drug abuse."

Item 3:

(From *The Independent Alligator,* University of Florida):

When Florida college students are missed by the U.S. census, the state loses federal funds and potential congressional seats.

Therefore, state officials are saying they will try to do something about it.

There are nine public universities and 28 community colleges in Florida. Students attending these institutions make up about 7.5 percent of the state's population, but they are usually under-represented in census courts, said State University System Spokesman Pat Riordan on Monday.

The census is done predominantly through questionnaires that are sent to every known address in the country, including college dormitories. Mailings that aren't answered are followed up by phone calls and door-to-door visits by census workers. The entire information gathering process takes about three years.

Riordan said college students slip through the 10-year population count (with the next one coming up in March) because they keep odd hours and sometimes try to escape government intrusion into their lives.

Here's Riordan's quote: "Each person costs the state money through the services they use—either by using the highway, using health services, the judicial system, public schools, whatever—and we get money from the federal government to help pay for those services. But if someone isn't counted, we aren't given money for them."

On student unavailability, he said this: "They're not home at convenient times to receive phone calls or visits from census workers. You know, they're not around from eight to five, and making appointments with them is not always easy. Also, some people avoid any government attention, either because they like their privacy or because they don't pay taxes, or whatever. We'll be trying to let college students know that this is not some kind of harassment, but it's an important thing that helps the state."

College students are not the only group undercounted. Other groups traditionally under-represented in the census are the homeless and young black males.

Last week Gov. Bob Martinez said that the state's growth in the 1980s could result in as many as four new seats in Congress and billions of federal dollars. The governor appointed the Complete Count Committee last year to improve census accuracy. He said each Florida resident who isn't counted costs the state $300 a year in federal funds.

Riordan said the State University System is cooperating with the count committee and will be heading a media campaign to educate college students on the fiscal advantages of the census.

Here's his quote on that: "The reason the SUS is concerned is because the funds we rely upon are often based on population. Right now, we get back 85 cents of every dollar Florida residents pay into the federal government. The more people we have in the state, the more of that dollar we'll get."

ASSIGNMENT 10.13

In the following quotations taken from published college student newspapers, discuss the verb of attribution used with the direct and indirect quotes. If you disagree with its use, change it.

1. Giest said he believes the experience he gains in the next three years will help him in the future.

"If I intend on entering the restaurant industry when I graduate, working for Marriott will look great on my resume and the experience will help me compete in the market," claimed Giest.

2. There are required courses for admission to medical school, but you do not have to declare yourself a pre-med major. The pre-medical department exists to assist students in fulfilling their undergraduate and professional admission requirements. They help to organize students' undergraduate studies.

"You have to be ready for hardship," according to Anton Seafini, a senior.

3. Another effect of the rain forest destruction is shifting monsoon patterns. The annual monsoons, known throughout history in Southwest Asia, have failed to appear for the past three consecutive years, according to Solochana Gadgill, a meteorological expert in India.

"The world's future climate depends on the halting of this insane destruction," warns Burman of the National Academy of Sciences.

4. Harrison has also noticed a high deficiency in students' English grammar skills.

"There isn't as much of that taught in the schools as there used to be," he explained. "It's a problem that probably started back in the '70s, but it's never been corrected."

5. Working with the Food and Drug Administration and the World Health Organization, the Commission creates international guidelines and standards since "there are big differences between the western countries and most Third World countries," Levy explained.

6. "It's going to be an incredible event, one of the classiest events to hit this campus in years," gushed Nancy Cleminshaw, of the sponsoring UW Alumni Association.

ASSIGNMENT 10.14

Conduct a telephone interview. Before doing so, contact your source, either in person or by phone, to arrange a time and date for the telephone interview. You may explain that the interview should take about 10 to 15 minutes. In advance of the interview, write at least 10 questions that you will ask your source. Have your instructor read over questions to give you suggestions.

After you have completed the telephone interview, type up your notes and bring them to class.

ASSIGNMENT 10.15

Read the following story from the University of Florida's *Independent Alligator*. Discuss identification of sources. Then, referring to the six guidelines in using direct quotations and natural sound in news writing on pages 208 and 209 in the textbook, discuss how this story illustrates or ignores those suggestions.

NEWSPAPER: *The Independent Alligator,* University of Florida
DATE: Wednesday, November 22, 1989
VOL. 83, NO. 63
HEADLINE: 'The Lord provides it, and we cook it'
PAGE: 8

It's easy to find Thelma Markham at Thanksgiving. Just pull up next to the Grove Park store on Highway 20 east of Gainesville, roll down the window and ask for T.J. One of the many locals who gather around the picnic table will point east and say, "Just follow your nose."

The brief directions are explicit indeed. If Thelma is home and the wind is blowing the right way, the delectable scent of roasting wild meat will mingle with the aroma of fresh vegetables and attract hungry visitors from all over town.

Down the pitted dirt road that leads to Thelma's place, the modern world temporarily ceases to exist. On both sides of the road, amid the trees draped with Spanish moss, stand multi-colored houses arranged helter-skelter like handfuls of tin-roofed dice thrown down by some impetuous gambler.

It's easy to distinguish Thelma's house from the rest. The laughter there is louder, the crowd larger and the welcome heartier.

"Pick up a plate and sit down," is a favorite greeting of Cheristine, Thelma's sister. She will tell you in a friendly bluffness to go into the dining room and fill up your dish.

The food will be in a horseshoe-shaped arrangement in the rustic dining room. But filling your plate may not be an easy task; at any time there might be 40 or more of Thelma's friends and relatives vying for the steaming foods in the compact room. If this is the case, then it is a perfect time to visit the cook.

Thelma, 26, will be in her small kitchen, adjacent to the dining room. She will greet you with a smile and talk to you as she skillfully prepares some of her specialties, ranging from cooter to 'coon and gator to gravy. Some opossums will be in the pot and turkeys in the oven as she wipes her hands with a towel and carries a casserole dish heaped with swamp cabbage into the awaiting holiday throng.

Thelma, who is single and has no children of her own, is the uncontested culinary master of her family. She has been for years.

But exactly how long ago she took command of the kitchen is uncertain.

"She was about 8 years old when she started," Thelma's uncle Johnny Mack, 40, said. Sitting on one of the two living room couches, wearing a grey Fedora and sipping a cold Old Milwaukee, Johnny reminisced about Thelma's earliest meals.

"I started cooking at least 18 years ago," Thelma said.

"She was 11. And the first thing she cooked was a red velvet cake," said Zennie Sheffield, Thelma's 80-year-old great-grandmother.

Although her family disagrees about when Thelma began her cooking, everyone agrees that her food is excellent.

"They better tell me my food is good. 'Cause if they don't, they won't be eating here anymore," Thelma said with determination.

For Thelma's family, having her in the kitchen means having a cornucopia on the table. But exactly how big is Thelma's family?

"I got so many grand, great-grand and greater-grandchildren that if they were all hogs, I'd be rich," Mrs. Sheffield said. "I came down here from Georgia about 45 years ago with my father and my five children. Now I have close to 100 relatives living around here."

Mrs. Sheffield lives in the house next to Thelma's. The two houses, along with the yard that separates and surrounds them, have a personality all their own. The yard is frequented and fertilized by an array of animals, domestic and wild.

Red and yellow hens and roosters, pecking and cock-a-doodling at whim, strut around the amber grass and green shrubs. Armadillo and wild turkeys sometimes venture on the grounds and usually find themselves on Thelma's table. Bunky the cat scampers around, evading the eight or nine dogs that wait not so patiently for a generous handout from Thelma. A black pig named Arnold rounds out the cast.

The cacophony created by those animals sometimes competes with other noises made by various children screaming and groups of men shooting their shotguns in preparation for the day's hunt.

"You should have been here this past Super Bowl," Johnny Mack said. "I brought home a 10-point deer." He spread his arms wide to show the breadth of the animal's antlers with the 10 horns. "It fed about 15 people."

Thelma opened up one of her family's five full-length freezers. It was as full as a supermarket's meat case. She started pulling out the frozen bundles to try and tell what each one contained. After scraping ice off of the basketball-sized chunks of meat, she began to tell what was in each plastic-wrapped package.

"This is some of that wild boar. This is rabbit. This is probably 'coon. I think this is some of that wild turkey. Hmmmmmm, I don't know what this is."

"All of our freezers are like that," Cheristine said as she sat at the table eating some of Thelma's fried opossum and sweet potatoes, garnished with red peppers. "We're prepared for anything—hurricanes, tornadoes, water flows, fire—you name it.

The hundreds of pounds of meat and vegetables tucked away in Thelma's freezers probably could feed the whole family every day for one month before the supply ran out. But the freezers are unlikely to become barren, because everybody constantly adds either animals or vegetables to the stockpile.

"My cousin, he's the one who gets me the swamp cabbage," Thelma said. "He goes down by the trestle where the fishing water is, and there are these pell-mell plants. He gets a machete and cuts away at the bark to the middle. Then he brings it to me. You have to cook it longer than regular cabbage though, just like you're cooking a pot of greens.

"Now my granddaddy, he has a garden with red peppers, greens, iced potatoes—just about all the vegetables we eat come from his garden. He's about 68 or 69 years old, and brother, he could sure get around. He's also cheaper on your pockets. All you have to do is go down there and bring him a six-pack, and he'll give you whatever you want."

With bartering like this, Thelma's table is seldom lacking in food, and this fact is never more obvious than at Thanksgiving.

The heat from the wood-burning stove banished the autumn cold and gave the house an old-world scent as Thelma sat at the dining-room table and told how she prepares her holiday banquets.

"In the evening, I start cooking. I'll cook until about five o'clock in the morning, and then I'll go take a nap.

"When I get up, I'll start putting out the food. It will be spread over that dresser, that dresser and this table." She made a sweeping motion with her hand around the room, showing the extent of the banquet area.

"Everybody starts at one end and works their way around. If they don't get enough the first time, they just have to go through the line again. Most people will come with their Tupperware dishes and take the food to go because there wouldn't be enough room for everybody if they stayed here."

The more than 40 guests who Thelma fed last Thanksgiving, however, found ample dining area in the yard and an overabundance of food on the table.

"I had ham, two turkeys, deer, opossum, 'coon. Let's see. Oh, yeah, I had a duck too. My nephew got it. My granddaddy gave us mustard and collard greens, string beans, potatoes, peas in the shell and okra. And we had swamp cabbage, too."

As if trying to establish the logic of it all, she said, "You see, you just can't have one or two meats at Thanksgiving or Christmas."

Her words came almost as an echo of her great-grandmother.

"If the children eat all that's there, there wasn't enough," Mrs. Sheffield said. "I brought them up that way."

To feed squadrons of hungry guests in the hearty manner that Thelma does, one would expect to pay dearly at the neighborhood supermarket.

"I gave my mother $50 to get some eggs, salt, pepper, milk and macaroni from the store," Thelma said. "Altogether I paid less than $40 for the Thanksgiving meal that lasted two days. The rest of the food was all natural. It came from out there." She pointed toward the dense woodland that sprawled behind her backyard.

Thelma's natural, robust personality is mirrored in the way she cooks her food. She abides by a no-frills code when preparing her meals. She has no need for exotic spices or arcane herbs. And she finds no need for a pencil and paper.

"A lot of people come along with a recipe book, and still their food don't taste good," Thelma said.

She went into the kitchen and came out with a one-quarter teaspoon silver measuring spoon. Then she dipped it into an imaginary canister, showing her spicing technique.

"I take a little spoon like this and I estimate. I judge a little bit. At times, I'll use parsley, bay leaves, paprika, seasoned salt, celery or oregano. I put whatever I want to put in."

She put down the spoon and picked up a three-inch bone from a plate.

"Could you tell this was once a opossum?" she asked smiling. "Let me tell you about opossum. First, you can't go reachin' in the trap and grab one out or you'll get bit. Then you'll have to make sure they aren't foamin' at the mouth or you'll get sick. Then you swivel them over an open flame to get the hair off of them. After that you wash them down with washing powder and let them sit in salted water for a while to get the burnt taste out."

Thelma has a similar technique for wild turkey. She also has tricks on how to take the wild out of wild rabbit and ways to tenderize even the most sinewy meats. Yet there remains some secrets she won't reveal.

"I don't go giving away all my recipes," she said.

Even if some of her recipes are sacrosanct, most of the pleasure is in the palate, not in the preparation. Except maybe for Thelma.

"Cooking is a wonderful experience," Thelma said with an air of satisfaction. "I enjoy cooking and knowing that everybody knows where they are going to eat. It's just like the Waltons. They say grace, hold hands, and especially bless the cook." She halted, and with arms akimbo, said, "If they don't, they'll get sick!"

Enthusiastically, Thelma went on to tell about her aspirations for a special kind of restaurant.

"I'm gonna have some of everything. I'll be open for breakfast, lunch and dinner and have two bodyguards because of the crime and stuff. And I'm gonna call it, 'The Soul Food and Wildlife Restaurant.' "

If only a fraction of Thelma's friends and family dine at her prospective restaurant, it will become a bonanza. But until then, her intimate clientele will continue its feasting and festivities at her home, realizing how good life can be.

"We do it good in the woods," Cheristine said as she enjoyed a piece of Thelma's wild rabbit. "The Lord provides it, and we cook it."

Reprinted with the permission of the *Independent Alligator*, University of Florida, Gainesville.

IV | WRITING ABOUT SPECIFIC SUBJECTS

11 | Speeches, Press Conferences, Meetings

Write a 500- to 750-word news story based on the commencement remarks by Jon Nordheimer, national correspondent for *The New York Times*, at the University of Miami School of Communication, December 1988. Nordheimer was speaking to the students at mid-year commencement held by the school. At the time, he was holder of the Knight Chair of Communication at the University of Miami:

GOOD AFTERNOON.

WHEN DEAN PFISTER INVITED ME TO MAKE SOME REMARKS AT THIS CEREMONY HE EMPHASIZED THEY SHOULD BE BRIEF.

HE KNOWS SOMETHING ABOUT NEWSPAPER WRITERS.

NOT MANY ARE GOOD SPEAKERS.

TOO MANY YEARS SITTING IN RELATIVE ANONYMITY. WE HIDE BEHIND THE MODEST WALL OF A BYLINE, INFORMING THE WORLD ABOUT THE WORLD, BUT LITTLE ABOUT OURSELVES IN THE PROCESS.

WE PRINT JOURNALISTS—THOSE OF US IN NEWSPAPERS, MAGAZINES AND OTHER FORMS OF PUBLISHED INFORMATION—COMMUNICATE IN SECRET VOICES.

OUR READERS ARE GENERALLY NOT CONCERNED WITH WHAT WE LOOK LIKE. WHETHER WE ARE TALL OR SHORT, FAT OR THIN— IF WE MEN WEAR MUSTACHES OR GRAVY STAINED TIES OR THE WOMEN JOURNALISTS WEAR THEIR HAIR UP OR DOWN.

THE READER HOPEFULLY JUDGES US ON THE QUALITY OF THE FACTS WE PRESENT AND—PERHAPS—ON THE STYLE IN WHICH THE FACTS ARE PRESENTED. NOT HOW WE ARE PRESENTED.

THE PUBLIC RARELY HEAR OUR VOICES BECAUSE READING OUR WORDS REQUIRES THE READER TO LISTEN TO HIS OR HER OWN VOICE: TO REPEAT OUR PRINTED WORDS IN THEIR OWN INTERNAL

VOICE IN THE MICRO SECOND IT TAKES TO GO FROM THE EYE TO THE CEREBRAL CORTEX.

IF YOU DON'T BELIEVE ME TRY IT SOMETIME.

IT IS POSSIBLE TO HEAR SOUNDS WHILE PERFORMING OTHER TASKS—OR HAVE THE IMPRESSION THAT ONE IS LISTENING WHILE DOING SO. FOR EXAMPLE, THE HOUSEWIFE DOING THE IRONING WITH A SOAP OPERA ON THE TELEVISION IN THE BACKGROUND. BUT IT'S THE MOST PASSIVE INVOLVEMENT IN ACQUIRING INFORMATION. I DON'T BELIEVE IT'S POSSIBLE TO READ AND PERFORM OTHER TASKS. IT REQUIRES SOME LEVEL OF CONCENTRATION, PARTICULARLY IN THE REALM OF COMPLEX INFORMATION OR DIFFICULT IDEAS.

THIS SIMPLE PROCESS—READING WORDS IN PRINT AND UNCONSCIOUSLY OR SEMICONSCIOUSLY REPEATING THEM ALOUD IN THE MIND—IS AN ACT THAT CREATES A TRUST BETWEEN A READER AND A PIECE OF INFORMATION HE IS CONTEMPLATING, AND THIS SIMPLE ACT HAS BEEN THE ENGINE OF WESTERN CIVILIZATION FOR SEVERAL CENTURIES.

IT WAS VICTOR HUGO WHO SAID:

"THE INVENTION OF PRINTING WAS THE GREATEST EVENT IN HISTORY.

WHEN PUT INTO PRINT, THOUGHT IS MORE IMPERISHABLE THAN EVER. IT IS VOLATILE, INTANGIBLE, INDESTRUCTIBLE."

NOW, AS WE STAND IN THE FAINT LIGHT OF A NEW CENTURY THAT IS GLIMMERING JUST OVER THE HORIZON A SCANT DECADE AWAY, WE ARE AMUSED AND NOT A LITTLE BEFUDDLED OVER THE EXTENT TO WHICH TELEVISION AND ITS ASSOCIATED TECHNOLOGIES HAVE REVOLUTIONIZED THE WAY WE RECEIVE INFORMATION AND PERCEIVE IT.

WHAT WOULD VICTOR HUGO THINK OF THIS NEW TOOL AND ITS RELATION TO THOUGHT?

I BELIEVE HE WOULD DECLARE IT VOLATILE TO A FAULT. BUT I DON'T BELIEVE VICTOR HUGO WOULD BE QUICK TO DESCRIBE IT AS IMPERISHABLE.

AND I, FOR ONE, DON'T BELIEVE FOR A MOMENT THE REPORT THAT CAME OUT OF WASHINGTON THIS WEEK THAT A STUDY COMMISSIONED BY THE U.S. DEPARTMENT OF EDUCATION COULD NOT FIND SCIENTIFIC EVIDENCE TO SUPPORT THE COMMON BELIEF THAT CHILDREN'S HOMEWORK SUFFERS WHEN THEY DO IT WHILE WATCHING TELEVISION.

MORE ACCURATELY, I GUESS I BELIEVE THE REPORT THEY COULDN'T FIND THE EVIDENCE. BUT THAT'S NOT THE SAME AS SAYING IT'S NOT TRUE THAT HAVING THE BOX ON WHILE DURING HOMEWORK—OR LISTENING TO A HEAVY METAL BAND ON A WALKMAN'S EARPHONES—DOESN'T INTERFERE WITH LEARNING COMPLEX MATERIAL OR OVERLOAD THE MEMORY SYNAPSE IMPRESSED WITH FACT.

THE INVESTIGATORS DIDN'T DROP BY MY HOUSE. I HAVE TEEN-AGE CHILDREN. I'LL GIVE THEM FIRSTHAND EVIDENCE.

THE TELEVISION AGE, OF COURSE, DID NOT JUST SUDDENLY HAPPEN.

THE CHANGES HAVE BEEN UNDERWAY FOR A GENERATION OR SO. WHAT'S NEW IS THE DEPTH OF HOW IT IS CHANGING THE MANNER OF COMMUNICATING IDEAS AND HOW IT INTRUDES ON THE DISCOURSE BETWEEN CITIZEN AND ELECTED LEADER THAT JEFFERSON AND MADISON AND A HOST OF OTHER FOUNDING FATHERS ENVISIONED AS A FUNDAMENTAL REQUIREMENT TO KEEP THIS NATION FREE AND DEMOCRATIC.

THIS MUCH WE KNOW: TELEVISION GIVES US MORE INFORMATION ALL AT ONE TIME THAN WE CAN PROCESS AND ABSORB. THIS IS AS TRUE IN TELEVISION NEWS—PERHAPS MORE SO—THAN IN OTHER FORMS OF DAILY BROADCASTING.

THE PRESIDENTIAL CANDIDATE IS ON A PLATFORM GIVING A SPEECH.

THE WORDS TUMBLE OUT AND WE STRAIN TO UNDERSTAND THEM IF WE ARE DOING OUR DUTY AS CITIZENS.

BUT THE EYE IS BOMBARDED BY SO MUCH OTHER INFORMATION COMPETING FOR OUR ATTENTION.

THE CUT OR COLOR OF HIS SUIT OR SHIRT OR TIE.

THE WAY THE HAIR IS COMBED OR THE LACK OF HAIR. A SMILE. A RAISED EYEBROW. A GESTURE.

THE LOOK OF THE SUPPORTERS ON THE PLATFORM STANDING BEHIND HIM.

DO WE LIKE THEIR LOOKS OR COLOR OR FATNESS OR THINNESS? IN A TWINKLE THE JUDGMENTS ARE MADE, CONSCIOUSLY OR UNCONSCIOUSLY.

WHAT ABOUT THE REPORTERS ASKING QUESTIONS? DO WE LIKE THEM? WHAT IS THE TONE OF THEIR QUESTIONING?

IMPRESSIONS AND MORE IMPRESSIONS.

ALL WORKING TO BLUR WORDS AND THE THOUGHTS THE WORDS COMBINE TO REPRESENT.

DO WE, THE CITIZENS, BECOME VERY MUCH LIKE THAT PROVERBIAL HOUSEWIFE DOING THE IRONING WHILE THE BUZZ AND VISUAL DRONE OF TELEVISION BUMPS AROUND THE LIVING ROOM FOR A FEW MINUTES AND VANISHES INTO THE ETHER OR ENTERS OUR UNFOCUSED BRAINS MINIMALLY OR IN A DISORGANIZED FASHION?

IS IT NO WONDER THERE IS GREAT DISGUST ABOUT THE POLITICAL CAMPAIGNS AS THE CANDIDATES AND THEIR MANAGERS STRUGGLE TO SHAPE THESE IMPRESSIONS? TO BLUR EVEN FURTHER SOME IMAGES AND TO SHARPEN OTHERS?

IT WILL BE YOUR CHALLENGE AND YOUR DUTY—WHETHER YOU REMAIN IN COMMUNICATIONS AS A CAREER . . . OR WHETHER YOU SIMPLY CALL UPON THE SKILLS YOU HAVE LEARNED AT THIS UNI-

VERSITY—TO CUT THROUGH THE SOFTNESS OF THESE IMAGES IN A SOCIETY INCREASINGLY DEPENDENT ON TELEVISION FOR INFORMATION.

OR ELSE FACE EVEN GREATER DECAY IN THE BODY POLITIC AND THE DEMOCRATIC INSTITUTIONS THAT MADE THIS COUNTRY A BEACON OF POLITICAL FREEDOM TO THE WORLD.

THIS PAST NATIONAL ELECTION GIVES ONE PAUSE. THE WAY THINGS ARE GOING I AM BEGINNING TO BELIEVE THAT IN 1992 THE DEMOCRATIC PRESIDENTIAL NOMINATION WILL BE CONTESTED BY TED KOPPEL AND PHIL DONAHUE. WHILE THE REPUBLICAN FRONT-RUNNERS WILL BE GERALDO RIVERA AND MORTON DOWNEY JR.

OR IS IT THE OTHER WAY AROUND?

WHATEVER.

EVENTS IN THE WORLD MAY CONSPIRE TO MAKE THIS RESPONSIBILITY OF COMMUNICATING COMPLEX THOUGHT BY MEANS OF TELEVISION MORE DIFFICULT TO CARRY OUT THAN IT ALREADY IS. THE ONLY THING—HOPEFULLY—THAT WON'T CHANGE IS THE CITIZEN'S RESPONSIBILITY TO SUITABLY INFORM HIMSELF AND NOT BE MISLED. IT IS SOMETHING THAT CAN NEVER BE TAKEN AWAY FROM US. YET IT IS SOMETHING WE CAN ABANDON, AND PERHAPS ARE ALREADY IN THE PROCESS OF DOING. WE DON'T VOTE. YOUNG AMERICANS ESPECIALLY DON'T VOTE.

THIS CLASS OF GRADUATES—AS PROFESSIONAL COMMUNICATORS OR AS CONCERNED CITIZENS—FACE THE ENORMOUS CHALLENGE OF REFINING THE NEW TECHNOLOGIES—THEY WON'T JUST GO AWAY—AND ADAPT THEM TO THIS AMERICAN DEMOCRACY. IT WILL NOT BE EASY. FOR IT IS AGAINST A FAR MORE COMPLEX BACKGROUND THAN MERELY NEW FORMS OF COMMUNICATION AND RELATED PROBLEMS THAT AMERICANS AND THOSE IN THE COMMUNICATIONS INDUSTRY MUST STRUGGLE TO MAKE SENSE OUT OF THE TECHNOLOGICAL, SOCIAL AND POLITICAL CHANGES THAT SEEM TO REMAKE OUR LIVES EVERY FEW YEARS.

THE ADVANCE OF INFORMATION TECHNOLOGY IS COINCIDENTAL TO THE EXPLOSION OF OTHER TECHNOLOGIES THAT REVAMP OUR LIVES EVERY SEVERAL YEARS. IT USED TO BE THAT THE WORLD COULD PAUSE A GENERATION OR SO BETWEEN PROFOUND TECHNOLOGICAL ADVANCES OR A RESHAPING OF THE POLITICAL MAP THAT WEIGHED HEAVILY ON OUR LIVES. NOW IT SEEMS THE NEW GENERATION OF CHANGE HITS US EVERY FEW YEARS.

JUST AS WE ARE TOLD THIS CHRISTMAS THAT THE COMPACT DISCS WE PURCHASE WILL SOON BE MADE OBSOLETE BY DIGITAL TAPE RECORDINGS, AND OUR GIFTS GIVEN SO LOVINGLY WILL INEVITABLY END UP ON THE TRASH HEAP ALONG WITH OUR STEREOS AND HI-FI'S THAT WERE NEW AND BRIGHT AND SHINY JUST A FEW SHORT YEARS AGO—OTHER, MORE PROFOUND CHANGES CONFRONT US.

LOOK AT THE EVENTS OF THE PAST WEEK:

THE LEADER OF THE SOVIET UNION—VIRTUALLY IN THE SHADOW OF THE STATUE OF LIBERTY—ANNOUNCES UNILATERAL CUTS IN TROOP DEPLOYMENTS AND EXTENDS HIS HAND IN FRIENDSHIP AND ECONOMIC COOPERATION TO HIS NATION'S OLD IDEOLOGICAL ADVERSARIES. NOW ISN'T THAT A KICK IN THE PANTS FOR ANYONE IN EITHER OF THE TWO COUNTRIES RAISED IN THE BELIEF THAT ONLY ONE OR THE OTHER SYSTEM COULD SURVIVE— OR PERHAPS KILL EACH OTHER OFF?

IT'S TOO EARLY TO JUDGE THE SINCERITY OF GORBACHEV'S OVERTURES, AND RESISTANCE TO THIS NEW LINE MAY EVENTUALLY BE FAR MORE FORMIDABLE INSIDE THE SOVIET UNION THAN ANY REACTION FROM THESE SHORES. HE MAY HAVE TO FACE A POLITICAL EARTHQUAKE FAR MORE DEVASTATING THAN THE ONE IN ARMENIA THAT FORCED HIM TO CUT SHORT HIS TRIP TO AMERICA.

THESE ARE HUMPTY DUMPTY, ALICE-THROUGH-THE-LOOKING-GLASS TIMES FOR ANY AMERICAN WHO HAS SPENT MOST OF HIS OR HER LIFE LOCKED IN COLD WAR ORTHODOXIES. WE CAN EXPECT MORE BUMPS THAN SMOOTH PLACES ON THE ROAD TO THE FUTURE, AND YOU WHO PURSUE CAREERS IN JOURNALISM WILL BE CHALLENGED TO USE EVERY SKILL TO HELP AMERICANS DISCOVER THE TRUTHS ALONG THE WAY AND NOT BE LULLED INTO THE BLURRING OF FACT THAT HAS FOUND A PROMINENT PLACE IN THE WAY WE COMMUNICATE INFORMATION IN THIS SOCIETY.

IT IS A CHALLENGE THIS DEMOCRACY MUST CONFRONT, SO COUNT YOURSELF LUCKY THAT AS COMMUNICATORS YOU ARE BETTER PREPARED THAN MOST AMERICANS TO DO SOMETHING ABOUT IT.

AGAIN, CONGRATULATIONS ON YOUR ACHIEVEMENT AND GOOD LUCK IN THE FUTURE.

IT WASN'T TOO LONG AGO THAT AMERICANS OF CHRISTIAN HERITAGE WERE SOUNDLY CHASTISED FOR GOING TO CHURCH ONLY AT CHRISTMAS AND EASTER.

NOW MANY FAMILIES JUST GATHER THE KIDS AROUND THE TELEVISION SET IN THE PERIOD BEFORE THESE FOR WHAT IS NOW THE TRADITION OF WATCHING *IT'S A WONDERFUL LIFE* WITH JIMMY STEWART AT CHRISTMAS AND *THE WIZARD OF OZ* WITH JUDY GARLAND AT EASTERTIME.

I AM SURE IT HAS NOT ESCAPED YOU THAT BOTH FILMS DEAL BASICALLY WITH THE THEMES OF CHRISTMAS AND EASTER CONCERNING DEATH AND REBIRTH.

THE CHARACTER OF GEORGE BAILEY PLAYED BY JIMMY STEWART IS A DECENT DREAMER WHO BELIEVES HIS LIFE IS WORTHLESS, COMMITS SUICIDE AND IS MIRACULOUSLY RESURRECTED TO LEARN THAT HIS FAMILY AND HOME TOWN WERE VALUES WORTH LIVING FOR.

AND JUDY GARLAND IS TRANSPORTED BY THE DEADLY TOR-

NADO TO A HEAVEN-LIKE LAND WHERE SHE AND HER THREE NEW COMPANIONS LEARN THROUGH PERSONAL ORDEAL THAT THEY DO NOT REQUIRE MAGIC INCANTATIONS OF A WIZARD IN A PLACE NAMED EMERALD CITY TO FIND SALVATION.

THEY FIND COURAGE, WISDOM AND A CARING HEART ON THEIR OWN—REMEMBER THE LINE FROM THE 1970'S SONG—"OZ NEVER GAVE NOTHING TO THE TIN MAN/ THAT HE DIDN'T HAVE BEFORE" AND THEY GO ON TO DISCOVER THEY CAN FIND LOVE AND HAPPINESS ONLY AT HOME WITH THE PEOPLE THEY LOVE. THERE'S NO PLACE LIKE HOME—EVEN OVER THE RAINBOW DOESN'T COMPARE.

AND EVEN E.T.—THAT CELESTIAL WANDERER WHOM STEVEN SPIELBERG CREATED OUT OF PETER PAN AND NUMEROUS OTHER REVERED FIGURES IN OUR CULTURE—LONGED TO THE POINT OF DEATH TO RETURN . . . HOME . . .

IN A FEW YEARS AFTER THE CASSETTE SALES DECLINE I AM SURE E.T. WILL BE A STANDARD FIXTURE OF HALLOWEEN THOUGH, ON A CLOSER EXAMINATION OF THE MATERIAL, IT COULD EASILY FIT INTO THE CHRISTMAS OR EASTER LINEUPS.

IT IS INTERESTING TO NOTE THAT E.T., WHEN RELEASED IN 1982, WAS A BLOCKBUSTER AT THE BOX OFFICE, THE BIGGEST HIT EVER, AND *IT'S A WONDERFUL LIFE* AND *THE WIZARD OF OZ* WERE BOTH BOX OFFICE FAILURES WHEN ORIGINALLY RELEASED A GENERATION AGO WHEN HOME AND UNBROKEN FAMILIES WERE NOT THE CURIOSITIES THEY HAVE BECOME TODAY.

INTERACTION OF FANTASY AND REALITY IS NOT JUST PART OF OUR ENTERTAINMENT BUT ALSO THE BEDROCK OF CULTURAL MYTHS AS WELL. TODAY, THERE IS A HUNGER FOR NEW MYTHS, BUT UNTIL THEY COME ALONG WE TURN BACKWARD TO CONFIRM THE OLD ONES WORKED.

AS COMMUNICATORS, WE SHALL TRY TO KEEP OUR EYE ON REALITY AND SEPARATE IT FROM FANTASY, BUT ANYONE WHO TELLS YOU THE JOB IS GETTING EASIER HASN'T BEEN OBSERVING THE ACCELERATED PACE OF OUR SOCIETY AS IT BRAVELY PLUNGES HEADLONG INTO UNEXPLORED TERRITORIES OF THE MIND AND CULTURAL AND SCIENTIFIC EXPERIENCE.

Reprinted with the permission of Jon Nordheimer.

ASSIGNMENT 11.2

It is likely that there will be a speaker in the near future on your campus. Go to the speech and try to write a news story on what the speaker says. If this is not possible, check the cable television listings for C-Span I and II and write a story based on a speech broadcast by C-Span.

ASSIGNMENT 11.3

Using a reference source such as *Vital Speeches,* read a famous speech and write a story based on the transcription of the speech. Next, go to your library's microfilm files and find copies of how reporters covered the speech at the time it was given. For example, write a story on Abraham Lincoln's Gettysburg Address and then check how New York and Washington newspapers covered it. Are there differences in your story and the published ones? Why?

ASSIGNMENT 11.4

Call your city or county government center and ask for the time, date, and place of the next city or county government meeting. Attend the meeting and take notes. Write a story about what you see and hear. Compare your story the next day with the one published in your local newspaper. How are the two stories similar? How are they different?

ASSIGNMENT 11.5

Get a copy of the city or county agenda for the meeting you decided to attend in Assignment 11.4. Select an item that interests you. Report the story for background information only. This could include quotes from sources you interview in advance of the meeting.

Write the background (some newspapers call this B matter) as if you were going to turn it in for publication. If you attend the meeting, include the fresh information as the lead for the background information you provided.

ASSIGNMENT 11.6

Check your local cable television system to see if it offers Cable News Network, C-Span, or a similar 24-hour broadcast news service. Check regularly on this channel for press conferences involving breaking news stories. Watch one of these and try to write a story from what you see and hear.

ASSIGNMENT 11.7

The mayor of your city is expected to announce tomorrow that he/she will be running for governor. You are assigned the story.

Research the "B matter" (excluding quotes, since this is a fictional assignment). This background should be partly biographical with heavy emphasis on the mayor's political career. It also should include the current governor and information on him or her.

ASSIGNMENT 11.8

The following is a press release from the Vice President, Office of the Press Secretary. You are given this release in advance of the vice president's remarks. Then-Vice President George Bush was being honored by African-Americans (mostly businessmen) at a special dinner in Washington. The gathering was an endorsement of Bush's bid for the presidency. (Applause is indicated in parenthesis).

You are assigned to write a 500-word story on this speech. Be sure to check any unfamiliar terms or references.

PRESS RELEASE
THE VICE PRESIDENT
Office of the Press Secretary

FOR IMMEDIATE RELEASE   CONTACT: 202/456–6772
Monday, March 21, 1988

EXCERPTS OF REMARKS FOR
VICE PRESIDENT GEORGE BUSH
BLACK AMERICANS SALUTE TO GEORGE BUSH
WASHINGTON, D.C.

When I was in New Jersey today, I'm happy to say, I picked up the support of Governor Tom Kean. He has done a remarkable job of reaching out not only to fellow Republicans, but to traditional Democrats—black voters in particular. His success is an inspiration for what we can accomplish nationally as a party.

Tom Kean is one of the nation's most successful and popular governors. There's a reason for that. He's not just an outstanding governor . . . he's an outstanding politician. He symbolizes what we must strive for—the politics of inclusion.

If I am the Republican nominee, and I believe I will be, I want to attract to this party, the party of Lincoln, the broadest base of Americans possible . . . and that includes blacks, Hispanics, and all minorities.

And why not? We are the party of hope and opportunity. We are the party of economic growth and freedom. If I'm elected President, my administration will stand for better educational opportunity, more training, better jobs. We must help those who are trapped in poverty break out and break free. (Applause).

There are principles that our party should stand for, and that is why as National Chairman, with the help of Art Fletcher, Stan Scott, and so many others, we worked to open the Republican Party's door to all minorities. And under a Bush Administration, opening up the party to all will be a key priority.

Success in government and politics calls for straight talk, the establishment of principled objectives, and the courage to lead. The future of our nation depends almost solely on how well educated are our young people, how disciplined they are, what values they hold, and what ideals they establish as standards to lead America. And it all begins with basics.

I believe that everyone should have a chance to take part in all that's good about this country. I believe any individual should be able to rise and prosper on the basis of talent and grit. I believe everyone should have an equal place at the starting line.

The starting line begins with education. Our children need schools where they can learn . . . places where discipline is in and drugs are out . . . places where they will acquire not just the knowledge but the values that will prepare them for the future.

We should demand more from students—higher academic standards, with more emphasis on core courses like English, math, science, and history—and more homework. We should test students, early and often, to make sure they are learning what they should. We should put a stop to automatic promotion and graduation. (Applause).

By demanding these things, we will provide more opportunity . . . for all students, but particularly for those who have the farthest to go—because the poor are not served by meaningless diplomas. They are served by real preparation for the real demands of real life.

At the same time, we should provide more—more support for Head Start, and more assistance to the disadvantaged through Chapter I. We can reach more than 80 percent of the black children in this country by targeting just four percent of the school districts.

(Mr. Bush strayed from prepared text here to refer to his wife Barbara, who has adopted illiteracy as a project). And we should undertake a major assault on illiteracy. Every kid in America should be able to read and speak English.

Will this be expensive? Well, consider this: The chairman of Xerox estimates that businesses spend $25 billion each year to train workers who "can't read, can't write, and can't count." The best investment we can make is in our children.

Coupled with education is the necessity of teaching values—values of respect, of faith and family. There is nothing as important as the family structure to a child looking for stability, guidance, example. These values must be inculcated into our children not just in school, but in our churches, our communities, and especially in our homes.

And we must lead our nation in this direction.

And where family is split, divided, federal law must insist that the absent parent fulfill his responsibilities to his kids and spouse.

And where family is so weak that a kid literally has no chance at home, we must support programs like Cities in Schools; we must support good teachers, good principals, so that every kid has someone who knows his name—who really cares.

Coupled with the importance of education is the protection of your freedom . . . your civil rights.

To me, this is not just a matter of social policy, but of fundamental right—the inherent equality of all men and women. "Who we are as a people can be measured by how we uphold and defend the rights of all. And it is our willingness to respect these rights even when it is difficult that sets America apart from every other nation on Earth.

I will have a positive civil rights agenda. I guarantee you, I will personally get involved in protecting the civil rights of every American. This effort will be at the top of the agenda of my attorney general, and he or she will be directly accountable to me for results.

Let me be very frank with you: The legislation on Grove City is imperfect, and the imperfections should be corrected. Having said that, however, the federal government must require that organizations that get tax dollars comply with our civil rights laws. That's fundamental. (Standing ovation).

But just protecting civil rights does not assure equality of economic opportunity. We must knock down the walls of indifference and other barriers that result in economic exclusion.

Our society—historically, politically, and economically—is built on inclusion. We have grown to greatness precisely because we have accepted the contribution of all who have come to our shores.

Now we need to bring in those who are already here, but who have been left out. We must bring black Americans and other minorities into the free enterprise system, into the government, into the Republican Party—not just because it is right, but because it is good for us—all of us. (Applause).

As we prepare for the year 2000, America will have to field a full team if we're going to remain competitive. It's not just in the interest of blacks . . . it's not just in the interest of Hispanics . . . it's not just in the interest of women . . . it's in the interest of America to help economically empower all.

A strong and growing economy is the key to this effort . . . one that turns loose the power of the private sector to create jobs and new opportunities.

We have turned that power loose in this Administration, and the result is more than 15 million new jobs since the recovery began. The longest peacetime expansion ever. Inflation down. Interest rates down. Personal income up.

Some would have you believe that only the rich have prospered. That's nonsense. We've seen explosive growth in the black middle class. A third of all black families today earn more than $25,000 a year. But these gains are fragile, and there's much more left to do.

It's been nearly 20 years since President Nixon issued an executive order to establish the Office of Minority Business Enterprise at the Commerce Department. In the years ahead, I aim to restore and reinvigorate the vision that originally led to the creation of OMBE. (Applause)

I want to help more black Americans and other minorities experience the pride and dignity of ownership, of building something in the private sector.

Government cannot do it alone. But government certainly can lead in this area. Government can work with the private sector to provide technical assistance, loan guarantees, and new capital sources.

A Bush Administration will help build the bridge of capitalism and entrepreneurship to the black community. Let's commit ourselves tonight to building that bridge.

I was a businessman before I was a politician. I started a business from scratch, and I know how tough it can be to take risks, to meet a payroll, to produce. But you know that. You've been out there on the cutting edge—getting the job done; providing opportunity for others.

You can tell me what we need to do to even up the odds, to help you get the access to the money and the people that can get new businesses off the ground.

What I am saying tonight—to those of you have the courage and the conviction to be with me tonight and to stand with the Republican Party—and I know it hasn't always been easy—what I'm saying tonight is that I will listen. In my Administration, I will have high-level black and minority men and women of excellence to tell it as it is—to help me understand, to help me lead.

To reach these goals, I will need your help and the help of all black Americans. You will be called upon, and you will be heard. By working together—and only by working together—we can finally achieve the dream of one nation, under God, with liberty and justice for all. We can make America truly free.

Thank you very much. (Standing ovation).

Reprinted with the permission of The White House, Washington.

ASSIGNMENT 11.9

Here are three listings from the "Happenings" column of the University of Miami student newspaper, *The Miami Hurricane:*

• The campus chapter of Amnesty International meets at 7:30 p.m. every Tuesday in Dr. Ken Smith's apartment, in Mahoney Residential College. For more information, contact Amy Young at 284–3684.

• The Organization of Jewish Students invites students to hear Janet Argan discuss "Planning the Perfect Summer: Avoiding Conflict" at 3:30 p.m. today in Hillel Jewish Student Center, 1100 Stanford Drive. For more information, contact Linda Levin at 665–6948.

• The Honors Students' Association will meet at 3:30 p.m. today in the Flamingo Ballroom, sections A, B, and C. Elections for secretary and historian will be held. For more information, contact Anh-Dao Le at 279–9713.

Find similar listings in your campus newspaper, or check school bulletin/information boards on campus for notices of meetings and upcoming events. Plan to attend one of these campus meetings. You will produce two stories.

(1) Advance meeting story. Write a short story (longer than the briefs illustrated above) to inform readers about the highlights of the agenda for the meeting. You must interview someone, preferably an officer, associated with the organization or club. If the meeting will feature a speaker, as shown in the third example, Organization of Jewish Students, try to interview the speaker by telephone to get the gist of what he or she will talk about. Be sure to include a little history about the organization (how many members, when it started, goals for the year, and so forth).

(2) Cover the meeting and write a story. You are allowed to use some material/information from the advance meeting story you wrote earlier.

ASSIGNMENT 11.10

Read the following speech story published in *The GW Hatchet* at George Washington University. Based ONLY on what you have read in this story, answer these questions.

1. What is President Bush's stance on the defense budget?
2. How old is McGovern?
3. What state did McGovern represent?
4. How long did he serve as senator?
5. What is the former senator doing now?
6. What is McGovern's political affiliation?
7. McGovern addressed several issues during his speech. What are they?

In addition to the Bush defense budget and the Soviet threat, the article mentions the following: ozone depletion of CFCs, drug problem, lack of leadership in the Democratic Party, the Rev. Jesse Jackson's political career. Find each of these issues in the story and discuss the transitional device (or lack of one) used to move the reader from one point to the next.

NEWSPAPER NAME: *The GW Hatchet*, George Washington University
DATE: Thursday, February 8, 1990
VOL.: 86, NO.: 36
HEADLINE: McGovern urges defense cuts to reduce U.S. budget deficit

Former Senator George McGovern attacked the Bush Administration's stance on the defense budget and said the $307 billion presently allocated to defense should be reduced and redistributed.

"The security threat to the United States is greatly reduced," McGovern said before a crowd of approximately 300 last night in the Marvin Center ballroom at the Program Board sponsored event. He added that the probability of a Soviet invasion is comparable to "an invasion from Mars."

McGovern said the reduction in the Soviet threat of a European invasion should be capitalized on. A peace dividend has been created by a reduction in military spending, according to McGovern, and should go towards both reducing the deficit and rebuilding the nation.

"When you walk out on the streets of any large city in the United States you don't worry about a Russian hitting you over the head," McGovern said. He added that the United States must think less about military dominance and concentrate more on economic stability.

McGovern said that the United States must deviate from taking a unilateral approach toward global problems and act multilaterally by involving other countries. "These go-it-alone tactics no longer fit the needs of our world," McGovern said.

When asked if he would support a unilateral bill calling for the reduction of ozone depleting chlorofluorocarbons (CFCs), McGovern said he would back any legislation that would combat the problem. He added, however, that CFCs are a global problem which will cease only if the international community gets involved.

"I would hope that the international community would really turn the screws" on countries that do not cooperate on the CFC problem, he said.

Pressuring countries that do not cooperate in solving environmental problems should be considered as important as pressuring countries who deny human rights, McGovern said.

As far as the drug problem is concerned, he noted, Drug Czar William Bennett is focusing too much on trying to curb the supply side of the problem.

"As long as you have a $200 billion (drug) market, a drug policy based on dealing with supply is doomed to failure," he said. "I would put the focus on the U.S. rather than on Panama, Colombia, or Peru."

McGovern called legalization of drugs a "possibility" but added he would not personally endorse such measures. "It is something that has to be carefully evaluated," he said. "It almost looks like an endorsement for drugs if you're not careful."

McGovern criticized the Democratic Party for not clearly defining an alternative for the United States in the past decade. He said he is disappointed that the party has not taken a more courageous stand and provided leadership.

On the local front, McGovern said the Rev. Jesse Jackson would not lose his political career if he were elected mayor of Washington D.C. "I don't think being mayor of Washington buries you," he said. "He'd get publicity all over the nation."

McGovern has not completely ruled out the possibility of running for president for yet a third time. "Well, I'm always considering.

"I guess every four years I have that temptation," he said.

ASSIGNMENT 11.11

Read the following news coverage by the student and professional press of a Boris Yeltsin speech during a recent U.S. visit. Write a short essay comparing the two stories. In your paper, address the following items: effectiveness of the lead, Yeltsin's political background, and the description of the political situation in the Soviet Union.

Then, based ONLY on what you have read in this story, answer these questions.

1. What is the Congress of People's Deputies?
2. Gorbachev's first name?
3. Identify Gorbachev.
4. How did Yeltsin "redefine the concept of a landslide?"
5. Was the event sponsored by the Graduate School of International Studies Institute *for* Soviet and East European Studies, or by the Institute of Soviet and East European of the Graduate School *of* International Studies.

NEWSPAPER: *The Miami Hurricane*, University of Miami
DATE: Tuesday, September 19, 1989
VOL.: 67, NO.: 6
HEADLINE: Radical Soviet calls for change
PAGE: 1

Amidst a mob of television reporters, photographers and well-wishers, Soviet politician Boris Yeltsin entered the banquet room of the Omni International Hotel Sunday and immediately began to work the crowd.

While his every movement was captured on camera, Yeltsin shook hands and smiled in the style of a true politician, while his interpreter explained to him what was happening.

Yeltsin later told the group, which consisted of such local notables as Miami Mayor Xavier Suarez and Miami Herald publisher David Lawrence, he has nothing good to say about conservative members of the Politburo, which he was moved from in 1987.

"Especially because they are trying to destroy Yeltsin," he said through interpreter Harry Colter.

In the 2,250-member Congress of People's Deputies, Yeltsin is leader of the Independent Caucus, which is a radical reform movement that started with 200 members in March and has grown to about 600 representatives.

A general constitutional overhaul is needed, according to Yeltsin.

The overhaul would include ownership for workers of this land, Politburo accountability to the congress and freedom to secede from the U.S.S.R. for the Baltic republics.

Additionally, Yeltsin said he thinks a radical bilateral reduction in arms, private ownership of a portion of the means of production and a socialist-based economy would benefit his country.

Yeltsin stressed the need for stronger relations between the United States and the Soviet Union.

"We have to pass over to a policy of speaking the truth," said Yeltsin. He said he came to speak the truth cause "the more truth we speak to one another, the greater will be the confidence" between our countries.

Yeltsin said glasnost, Gorbachev's policy of openness, must continue, as well as attempts to democratize the electoral process. He predicted Soviet citizens will someday enjoy nearly the same degree of freedom of choice in elections as Americans do.

"Yes, it's true we have had the first more or less democratic election to the People's Congress of Deputies.

"We have to carry through to the finish the political reforms started, which have already given us the nervous jitters," said Yeltsin.

Yeltsin reportedly received $25,000 for the engagement, which was sponsored by the Graduate School of International Studies Institute for Soviet and East European Studies.

When questioned about the fee, Yeltsin said if any of the money was left over after expenses, it would be used to purchase hypodermic needles for distribution to fight the spread of AIDS in his country.

Suarez said he was impressed by Yeltsin's straightforward, meet-the-press style.

"I have to say, Mr. Yeltsin," Suarez said, "that the way you were shaking hands and the way you have already redefined the concept of a landslide . . . it kind of makes me wish I had the same ability as I face reelection."

Dr. Bernard Schechterman, of the UM politics and public affairs department, said he was amazed at Yeltsin's showmanship.

"He should run for Congress here," Schechterman said.

The event was sponsored by the Institute of Soviet and East European Studies of the Graduate School of International Studies.

Reprinted with the permission of *The Miami Hurricane*, University of Miami.

NEWSPAPER: *The Miami Herald*
DATE: Monday, September 18, 1989
HEADLINE: Soviet urges democracy at home
AUTHOR/REPORTER: Luis Feldstein Soto
TITLE: Herald Staff Writer
PAGE: 1A

Maverick Soviet politician Boris Yeltsin, winding up his eight-day tour of the United States, serenaded Miami's anti-Communist ears Sunday by scolding his country's ideological hard-liners and egging them on to more private enterprise and democratic reforms.

Yeltsin displayed the tact of a politician and the wit of a stand-up comic in the final stop of his 11-city tour.

In measured tones that belied his fiery rhetoric, Yeltsin repeatedly tweaked the Soviet Union's ruling Politburo for its "machinations" against glasnost and perestroika, the country's twin movements toward political and economic freedom.

He even called for the ouster of five Politburo conservatives, beginning with his nemesis, hard-liner Yegor Ligachev.

"The first two years of perestroika had an enormous impact," said Yeltsin, the Soviet Union's leading populist politician. "They restored to the Soviet citizens that dignity which has been trampled for so many years. . . . People started thinking for themselves and stopped thinking exactly as their leaders thought, which was the case in our country for so long."

All day, the towering, silver-haired Yeltsin inspired laughter and awe for his constant, often humorous, jabs at the Soviet system. After spending Saturday night at Bal Harbour's Sea View Hotel, he crisscrossed Miami in a white stretch limousine that took him from a tiny Russian Orthodox church to a university professor's home and finally to a $100-a-plate luncheon at the Omni International Hotel.

For two hours, Yeltsin mesmerized about 500 listeners with his irreverent barbs at political opponents back home, including Soviet leader Mikhail Gorbachev. He called for "genuine political sovereignty and independence" for the U.S.S.R.'s republics, including the separatist-minded Baltic states, and for internal curbs on the power of the Communist Party.

The party should be treated like any other political organization and be "called to account" for any excesses, he said. Only then can the Congress of People's Deputies, to which Yeltsin was overwhelmingly elected last March, replace the Politburo as "the chief organ of power."

"This is particularly necessary in view of the fact that the Politburo today is leaning too far to the right and is pulling Gorbachev along with it," Yeltsin said.

In contrast, Yeltsin praised the American system, saying his visit had erased his childhood vision of Americans as "generally crude and offensive." He hailed everything from American democracy to American agricultural techniques—and, "of course, we shouldn't forget the beautiful American women whom we've met."

Yeltsin's message—that democracy isn't spreading fast enough back home—brought sober approval from both wings of Miami's often dueling Cuban exile leadership.

Jorge Mas Canosa, chairman of the fiercely anti-Communist Cuban American National Foundation, and Pedro Ramon Lopez of the more moderate Cuban Council for Democracy heartily applauded Yeltsin while ignoring each other. They reveled in his colorful tirades against the Soviet leadership, economy and even labor unions—which, Yeltsin said, do nothing more than "distribute free passes to rest homes and vacation spots."

Mas Canosa said later he wished "there were three or four more Yeltsins in the Soviet Union."

"A few years ago I wouldn't be having lunch at the same table with a Russian official or under a Soviet flag. A few years ago, Cubans would have burned it," Mas Canosa said. "The guy has come here to reinforce his international prestige and status as a life insurance policy to survive politically—and physically—back in the U.S.S.R."

Yeltsin also inspired unity—this time against him—during an earlier, five-minute visit to St. Vladimir Russian Orthodox Church in Little Havana. As he shook hands with wary parishioners, several grilled him about religious repression in his Communist homeland.

Though an admitted "religious nonbeliever," Yeltsin, thoroughly the politician, explained his church visit this way:

"We tend to undervalue the role of the church, especially for its influence on people's morality. Whatever we have tried to do against religion in the U.S.S.R., one third of the population remain believers and, therefore, a politician in the U.S.S.R. has to consider that."

His gesture didn't win many converts among the church's 30 to 40 worshippers, most of them Russian emigres or descendants of emigres, and all of them rabidly anti-Soviet. They see Yeltsin as a propagandist for a regime that has driven Orthodox Russians underground.

"I don't buy that Yeltsin dog-and-pony act," said Alex McKeehan, 42, who runs a property management business. "Does he have to come all the way to America to find God? Russia has thousands of Churches. All they have to do is open them up."

At the Omni luncheon, sponsored by the University of Miami's Institute for Soviet and East European Studies, some women detected a male chauvinist streak in their guest speaker.

When the wife of institute director Jiri Valenta asked him about Soviet military strategy, Yelsin said, "I think, Virginia, that your husband, Dr. Valenta, knows a good deal more about Soviet military doctrine than I do, and I'm sure he can answer that question for you."

Another woman got this reply: "Come and talk directly to me about that in Moscow. My telephone number is 292–7273." Yeltsin's eyes then darted to a nearby table. "Don't worry about your wife. Nothing will happen to her."

Both brush-offs struck Dade School Board member Janet McAiley as sexist. "He needs to experience all the subtleties of freedom and enlightenment," she said.

Yeltsin, who said his $34,000 fee for the Miami trip would pay for AIDS research back home, left for Moscow Sunday night.

12 Accidents, Crime, Fire, Obituary News

Interview a city or county police officer or a county medical examiner. Or talk to someone else involved in law enforcement. Write a feature on the job the person does, the person, and what the person thinks of the work. Watch him or her at work. Spend a few hours with the individual on the job if it is possible. How does the work fit into the overall law enforcement picture?

This story should run 3–4 pages, double-spaced.

ASSIGNMENT 12.2

Locate and interview the recent victim of a crime. Victims of holdups, such as service station attendants or quick-mart clerks, are best. Arrange the interview at your convenience, but try to locate someone within a week of the incident. Get the details from the police department and the D.A.'s office. Get the complaint document. Be detailed. Talk to witnesses.

Write 2–3 pages, double-spaced.

ASSIGNMENT 12.3

Interview a court official in person. This might be a judge, an attorney, a clerk, or someone else involved in the judicial process. Write a feature on their job, their work, and what they think about it. Watch them at work. Spend a few hours with the individual on the job if it is possible. How does the work fit into the overall law enforcement picture?

This story should run 2–3 pages, double-spaced.

ASSIGNMENT 12.4

Cover a trial. It need not be a complete trial. Set aside a block of time and attend a session of a trial. Write the story about that portion of the trial.

Select a trial in the county criminal courts. Ask the clerk of courts for assistance in selecting something interesting if you are unsure. A civil case at the county courthouse might be appealing. Be selective. If a decision or judgment is made, get the results and reactions from the principals.

Write 2–3 pages, double-spaced.

ASSIGNMENT 12.5

Interview a series of not less than a half dozen residents on a street or block in a neighborhood with a crime problem. These people must live in different households. If possible, select a neighborhood that has had a publicized problem. If you want help in locating one, just ask your local police department public information officer. Write a feature on the impact crime has on a neighborhood— look at the sociological and psychological impacts. Has it affected property values? The neighborhood economy?

Write 2–3 pages, double-spaced.

ASSIGNMENT 12.6

Investigate a court file on a completed case. It can be recent or several years old. Ask a court clerk to help you find an interesting case to study from the courthouse files. From the files, select one case and review it thoroughly. You can select, for example, a divorce case, a murder, or something else that appeals to you.

Try to find out what happened to the key people in the case. Write an update story. Where are they now? What are they doing now? Use your ingenuity in finding out. This assignment is rated "tough."

Write 3 pages or so, double-spaced.

ASSIGNMENT 12.7

You are a reporter for your campus newspaper. You are sitting around the newsroom today; there isn't much to do. Suddenly the phone rings and a staff member from the Public Affairs Office calls to tell you that your district's U.S. Representative died suddenly in his office in Washington while at work early today. Cause of death is apparent heart attack. He was found by his press secretary, name unavailable, at his desk at 9:15 a.m. Your school was notified by an alum working in an office down the hall in Washington.

The Congressman, you are told by the PR person, was a good and loyal friend of your school. Was he an alum? Check the files. The campus newspaper editor feels this calls for the page one lead story coverage, cutting out a story on lost library books. The only problem is that today is your deadline day for tomorrow's edition, and it will be going to press in two hours. She gives you the assignment:

Your class must divide into two groups. Each team should write one story on the death of this important public official and do it quickly. Write as much as you can, he says. Your editor says some research can be done on him if you hurry to the library. He suggests several sources off the top of his head, including the *Congressional Directory,* the staff in the local office of the Congressman, the coverage in your campus and your local newspapers during the most recent election campaign, microfilm in the library, politics and public affairs faculty at your school, a state almanac, and other directories and reference books.

ASSIGNMENT 12.8

Write a story from the following information. This story must be written for deadline today. If you determine that certain important information is missing, see your news source (your instructor). Use as much information as necessary. This is a major breaking story. More information is likely to be provided as you prepare the story. You are writing for the local afternoon newspaper or an evening newscast in Miami.

Your Notes

A tank car carrying chlorine gas has been cracked by a collision on a siding west of Hialeah, and the gas is seeping out of the tank. The Metro-Dade County Police office, which is responsible for the area outside the city limits, has ordered an evacuation of the area in which there are 15 residences with a total population of 70 persons. The accident occurred near NW 40th Street and NW 152nd Avenue.

The first word came at 6:20 a.m. from the Florida East Coast Railway Co., office in Miami, Sheriff John Pavlik says. One trainman was overcome by fumes, Albert Funster, 25, of Redding, Fla. He is in Hialeah Hospital where his condition is reported as not serious. The cause is unknown. What the train collided with is not known at this time either.

You check with the railroad and it estimates it will take no more than a few hours to remove the damaged car and transfer the chlorine to another tank car.

"We will put the families in a few motels, even if it is for a few hours," says the spokesman, Francis Praxton, of the local rail office.

As you prepare your story for the final edition, the police reporter calls you and says a family of four has just been taken to Hialeah Hospital in serious condition from chlorine inhalation. You call the hospital and learn their names: David Lewin, 35; his wife, Alice, 34; a son, Freddie, 7; and a daughter, Barbara 3. They live at 14918 NW 36th Street. They are in critical condition. A hospital official, Joan Deppa, says, "We understand there are several houses along there and that they are making a house-to-house search. I think the gas was seeping all night."

You call the railroad spokesman, and he verifies that they believe the accident occurred during some siding activity last night. You tell him about the family in the hospital. He has no comment.

You call the Metro police office again and ask about the search. Desk Sgt. Ernest Larkin confirms it. All available men have been sent to the area, and a contingent of Florida Highway Patrol—about a dozen—was sent out. The Red Cross emergency unit is there, and some Metro-Dade fire equipment, one fire truck.

As you, again, prepare to write, the police reporter calls and says a body, unidentified, has been removed from a house and taken to the Prewitt Mortuary in Sweetwater. It is a middle-aged woman. "We think there are more coming," he says. The house is at 14908 NW 36th Street. At this time, there is no ID on her and no confirmed cause of death.

You have no more time and must write. Remember there may be more information released later this morning as you prepare the story. It is believed a railway company spokesman will have a statement within the hour.

Your instructor will provide you with the statement when it becomes available.

ASSIGNMENT 12.9

With your instructor's assistance, invite a local police public information officer to speak to your class about police information reporting procedures. Ask your guest to bring copies of crime reports and investigation files for you to see.

ASSIGNMENT 12.10

From your local newspaper or from a local television newscast, clip or tape copies of emergency story news writing that contain too much legal or professional jargon to make sense to readers or viewers. How can these stories be improved? What definitions or explanations can be added?

ASSIGNMENT 12.11

Arrange to spend a part of a day or night with a team of local law enforcement officers to watch them work. As you do this, think about how you would write stories on each incident the officers investigate. Would these incidents be worthy of coverage? When you finish the observation, write a story about what you learned from the point of view of the officers.

ASSIGNMENT 12.12

Prepare an advance death story/obituary on your instructor or a member of your class. You will need to conduct research and arrange an interview with the individual. How will you write the lead without knowing the details of the death?

ASSIGNMENT 12.13

Five commuter students at your college or university have been injured in a two-car collision. Both of the drivers were students.

The accident occurred at 9 a.m. today at the main entrance of the campus. (You'll need to get the exact location and street names from your instructor.)

Today also is the first day of final exams. All students in the accident, you learn, were seniors.

Your campus newspaper editor (or campus radio station news director) sends you to the scene. You get there in time to see an ambulance driving off with two students.

Someone tells you they were the drivers of each of the cars.

Using the textbook's outline on Accident and Disaster News stories in chapter 12, specifically detail the facts that you would be looking for and key sources. Who would you interview first?

ASSIGNMENT 12.14

A fire is reported at your community's City Hall during the noon hour. Two reporters and a photographer from your city newspaper have been sent to the scene. You, however, have been asked to check for background on the building. You will feed this information to one of the two reporters when they return from the scene. What will you tell them?

Base your research on the following questions:

1. When was the building constructed (when did groundbreaking begin? When was the building completed? At what cost?

2. Any previous fires, accidents, criminal incidents at the building? When?

3. How much was the building worth before the fire?

4. How many city employees? How many are usually there in the afternoon?

5. Are there lunch or dining facilities in the building? Cafeteria? Vending machines? Both?

6. Get the name of the architectural firm and construction firm responsible for the building. Do they have a blueprint?

7. Has the building been altered since construction? (Additions, major renovations?)

8. Get the name of the maintenance or physical engineering supervisor.

9. Find out which meetings were scheduled at City Hall today.

10. Get any other interesting information about the building; it could be trivia.

ASSIGNMENT 12.15

Analyze the coverage of a national or international disaster in a major newspaper, or the local newspaper, within the past five years (for example, hurricanes, flash floods, blizzards, earthquakes). How many stories ran? How many sidebars?

Now, look at the main first-day story. What kind of lead and story organization did the story take?

ASSIGNMENT 12.16

Write your own obituary. Get quotations from teachers, friends, and relatives to include in the story.

ASSIGNMENT 12.17

Write an advance/prepared obituary of a famous person. This material will be the "B matter" since you do not know the details of the death at this time.

ASSIGNMENT 12.18

Analyze the obituaries of a famous person (Lucille Ball, Sammy Davis Jr., Gunnar Myrdal, James Baldwin, and so forth). Use two major newspapers or two news magazines for the analysis. Compare and contrast story organization and leads.

ASSIGNMENT 12.19

Here are notes for a story you will do on the stabbing of a 20-year-old University of Miami student:

Student is Christian Brogan, a UM junior.

He's in critical condition at Jackson Memorial Hospital.

Police are investigating the incident, which occurred Oct. 12.

Police say Brogan and his roommate, Sean McCarthy, 21, were attacked in the late evening as they left Sports Rock Cafe in South Miami's Bakery Centre. The cafe is a popular college hangout. The Bakery Centre is an enclosed mall about a half mile from campus. The cafe is on the top floor of the three-story mall. Before going to the cafe, Brogan and McCarthy had been at the UM Rathskeller, a campus pub.

Police reports said that a vehicle, which could have been a Ford Bronco or a Nissan Pathfinder, pulled up behind the car driven by McCarthy. McCarthy had stopped at the red light at the corner of Red and Bird roads. The two attackers got out of their car, dragged Brogan and McCarthy from their vehicle, and began to beat them.

McCarthy received several blows to the head and bruised ribs. He was not hospitalized.

Metro-Dade Homicide Detective Lou Alvarez: "We're just hoping that witnesses will come forward. That's our best hope." Alvarez said the attackers were described by witnesses as two white males in their twenties; one was wearing cowboy boots and had long, straight, dark hair.

More from Alvarez: "We are following up on some leads concerning the vehicle, but we need more information, either subject description or possibly a tag number. I believe there are people out there that were there, but haven't come forward." He said he is not sure of the motive of the attack, but: "We've traced where they (Brogan and McCarthy) were earlier in the evening, and there were no incidents at either location. Excluding any previous encounter, it's possible the attack could have been traffic-related. For example, they might have cut someone off."

McCarthy said he could not think of any incident in traffic that could have prompted the attack.

Brogan's mother, Noel: "According to the doctors, the best we can hope for, if he survives, is a vegetative, comatose state. The first 24 hours is the critical period after a major trauma like this, and there aren't any good signs."

Mrs. Brogan is staying with her husband, Conlin, at the apartment of one of her son's friends. Mrs. Brogan: "The president of the University [Edward Foote], Dean William Sandler, his English professor—they've all been so kind and feeling. Christian spread love wherever he went, and these beautiful people reflect that." She asked students or anyone with information to contact police: "At this point, every tiny bit is important. These animals are just going to prey on other college students."

Sari Golan has known Brogan for two and a half years and was a resident assistant on his residential college floor his freshman year: "I won't give up on him. Right now, I'm just hoping and praying. It's not fair for this to have happened to someone so young. All of his friends are trying to be there for him and lend support to his parents."

Brad Cole, a senior who has known Brogan for four years: "Everyone is hoping and praying that he's going to make it. He's an all-around super-nice guy who would've done anything for anyone.

He's the type of guy who would give you the shirt off his back if it were freezing."

ASSIGNMENT 12.20

Write a news story for a local newspaper or radio station based on the following information:

A former University of Miami football player has killed his former lover and then himself. Lucious Delegal, according to police reports, entered the South Miami post office parking lot, shot, and killed his former lover and mother of his son, then turned the gun on himself.

He was 28 and lived at 425 NW Sixth St. in Miami. His girlfriend was Regina Washington, a postal carrier working out of the South Miami post office. Police said the two apparently had been having problems with their relationship, and Washington, 24, wanted to end it.

She was shot in the head at close range and died instantly. Delegal, who also shot himself in the head, died later at Jackson Memorial Hospital.

Metro-Dade police said they did not know of any specific cause for the incident, but were still gathering evidence.

Delegal's past included burglary, theft, and four trips to reform school. He had managed to graduate from Norland High School in Miami after Allen Gainer, a juvenile probation officer, gained custody of the youth and gave him a sense of purpose.

Delegal went to Bethune-Cookman College in Daytona Beach, Florida, on scholarship, but transferred to UM after his sophomore year.

Delegal's first game as a part of the starting lineup was also his last in college. He played in the 1985 Fiesta Bowl game in UM's defensive backfield (UCLA defeated UM in the game).

Although he failed in a tryout for the National Football League, he did earn a degree in accounting from UM.

Those who knew him expressed great shock over the shooting and could not believe that he chose to throw away everything for which he had worked so hard.

13 Roundup, Aftermath, and Follow-Up Stories

ASSIGNMENT 13.1

From your local newspaper, clip three or four stories about news of your community. Take these stories and rewrite them into a single community news *Roundup* for a neighboring newspaper or a local radio station.

What item do you choose to lead with? How will you organize these stories? Don't forget to use transitions.

ASSIGNMENT 13.2

Find the back issues of your campus newspaper. They should be kept in bound files in the school library or newspaper newsroom.

Look back five or ten years ago and try to find a major news event that occurred which may have an anniversary in the near future. Develop an outline for an aftermath story on the event, using the old issues as background to suggest sources still on campus.

Is there anything new? How have the people involved changed? Do they view events differently now? Submit your outline for the story and list sources you will use. Also list questions you would ask. If you have the time, try to write the story.

ASSIGNMENT 13.3

Identify a breaking story today in your local newspaper or on one of the local radio or television newscasts. Think about how the story can be followed-up for the next issue or broadcast. What new information is needed? What sources are required?

ASSIGNMENT 13.4

In Assignment 12.19 you wrote a story about the stabbing of a University of Miami student. The information you used for your assignment was taken from one of three stories published in *The Miami Hurricane* on this tragedy. The following is the first-day or breaking story. Read it and compare the information in both stories. How much information from the first-day story is used in the follow-up story? What was new in the follow-up story?

NEWSPAPER: *The Miami Hurricane,* University of Miami
DATE: Tuesday, Oct. 17, 1989
HEADLINE: Two students assaulted, Stab victim in critical condition
PAGE: 1

University of Miami junior Christian Brogan, 20, was listed at Jackson Memorial Hospital after receiving a stab wound to the heart late Thursday night.

No further information on his condition was available Monday.

Hospital officials said his family had requested that no information be given out.

Police still have no clues to the assailants' identities.

Brogan and his roommate, senior Sean McCarthy, 21, were driving home from the Sports Rock Cafe in the Bakery Centre when the attack occurred. McCarthy received several blows to the head with a baseball bat and suffered bruised ribs but was not hospitalized.

Police said a Ford Bronco drove up behind the students and flashed its high-beam headlights in their rearview mirror.

McCarthy stopped the car at the corner of Red and Bird roads, apparently believing it was someone he knew, Metro-Dade police said.

Two white males got out of the Bronco, dragged Brogan and McCarthy from the car and began to beat them, police said.

McCarthy said he does not know what prompted the attack.

"The police are not really saying anything," he said.

However, McCarthy said police told him the attack could have been the result of words exchanged at the club.

McCarthy said he blacked out during the attack and does not remember getting hit.

"If they (the attackers) were standing right in front of me, I wouldn't know," he said.

The attack was interrupted when another car pulled up and began honking. The two attackers then jumped back in their Bronco and sped off, heading west on Bird Road, according to police.

Detectives are searching for a brown or red Ford Bronco, which is believed to be a newer model 4x4.

ASSIGNMENT 13.5

Here is information for the final follow-up story on the stabbing discussed in Assignments 12.19 and 13.4. Discuss the previous information from the earlier two stories and, along with this new information, write the final story:

Christian Brogan died Friday, Oct. 20, from a stab wound to the heart, Jackson Memorial Hospital officials said. The junior had been in a coma and listed in critical condition at Jackson for the past week.

Brogan was cremated Monday, Oct. 23. His ashes will be flown from Miami to New Jersey for the funeral. The funeral mass date has not been set, said his mother.

Police are still searching for evidence in the case.

Brogan's mother said she is concerned the attackers may try to hurt other UM students. She urged that everyone at the school should do whatever they could to prevent that from happening.

Here's quotable material from her: "The worst would be if Chris had died, and someone like this is allowed to prowl the streets. I would not wish this pain and agony on anybody."

ASSIGNMENT 13.6

Two employees of Miami-Dade Community College, North Campus, are retiring. One is Henry A. Thomas, a custodian who has worked at the campus for 18 years. The other is Anne Hays, who has been a secretary at the campus for 25 years. *The Falcon Times,* the campus newspaper, did separate stories on the two employees. Both of the stories are reprinted here. If the paper's editors had chosen to do so, the stories could have been combined for a round-up story on retiring employees. Read the two stories, and use the information to write a single round-up story. Each round-up item (one on Thomas, the other on Hays) should be no more than three paragraphs.

NEWSPAPER: *Falcon Times,* Miami-Dade Community College, North Campus
DATE: March 7, 1990
HEADLINE: Dade custodian Henry Thomas soon retires
PAGE: 6

The continuous smile, tractable eyes, and heavy-set body of Henry A. Thomas will not be seen around Miami Dade much longer.

Thomas, 65, who has been a custodian at the North Campus for 18 years, will retire next week (March 16).

"There's no particular reason I'm retiring," Thomas said, "except for the arthritis in my knee and my age."

Born and raised in Alabama, Thomas was a truck driver before landing his position at Miami-Dade.

Thomas' family consists of one son, Henry Jr., 30.

"He's a family man," said Delores Milton, custodian.

"Henry is always joking around; everyone loves him."

Milton, who has been a custodian at North Campus for 13 years, affectionately calls Thomas her "partner" while at work.

Through the 18 years Thomas has been at Miami-Dade, he has noticed many changes.

"A lot has changed since I've been here. Big improvements in working conditions and personnel have happened," said Thomas.

Thomas said he is sad about retiring, and will miss his co-workers and students most.

"I'll miss everything about Miami-Dade, but I am looking forward to having free time for traveling, fishing and hunting."

Reprinted with the permission of the *Falcon Times,* Miami-Dade Community College, North Campus, Miami.

NEWSPAPER: *Falcon Times*, Miami-Dade Community College, North Campus
DATE: March 7, 1990
HEADLINE: Co-workers say farewell to Anne Hays
PAGE: 6

Anne Hays received a grand send-off last week in the M.J. Taylor Lounge as the room was filled with co-workers to say goodbye to Hays, who has worked for Miami-Dade North for 25 years.

Hays joined Dade-North after 18 years of raising children and being a house-wife. She worked as secretary in various departments in the College. Hays' last position at Dade-North was as secretary for the associate dean of Social Sciences.

Hays started in the Registration office before there were computers. "All transcripts were pasted by hand," she said, "but we didn't make many mistakes."

Now that she's finished her career with Miami-Dade, Hays, a widow, plans to combine traveling with volunteer work. She said she'll miss her co-workers, but is looking forward to being away from routines and schedules.

Hays said she will take part in a literacy program and also be a listening grandmother for elementary students. She plans to visit Australia and the Scandinavian countries. "I want to enjoy my life," Hays said.

Nell Burns, Psychology professor, has worked with Hays for over 20 years. He has seen her grow into a "worldly, self-assured, aware, and liberated woman," he said.

Dr. J. Terence Kelly, vice president of the College, had an interesting story to remember Hays by. He said Hays was the only secretary he's had who "had a fistfight with another employee. Anne didn't start it, and I don't think she finished it."

Teary-eyed, Hays opened two gift-wrapped boxes. Her co-workers chipped in and bought her a double strand pearl necklace and matching pearl ring. "Barbara Bush will be envious," said Marilyn Runde, director of Student Activities.

ASSIGNMENT 13.7

Here is information from three stories published in the same edition (January 23, 1990) of *The Daily,* of the University of Washington (Seattle). You are assigned to write them into a round-up story. You are provided quite a bit of information for each item, but use only as much as you think is necessary. Before writing, decide which item is going to be your lead item. Be able to justify why you chose it.

Item 1:

The University of Washington's Department of Architecture will celebrate its 75th anniversary the weekend of Feb. 16–17. A number of events is scheduled to familiarize the public about the role architecture plays in society. All festivities are being sponsored by the UW Alumni Association.

Entire weekend festivities will cost $75; students, $25 for tickets purchased before Feb. 2.

The architecture department is one of four branches that make up the larger College of Architecture and Urban Planning. The Department of Architecture offers the only nationally accredited professional degree available in the field of architecture.

The planned events include an exhibit of alumni school work, a panel discussion and debate moderated by Professor Emeritus Norman Johnston, coordinated visits to the Seattle Art Museum's Frank Lloyd Wright exhibit, and campus walking tours.

The highlight of the weekend will be the "Beaux Arts Ball," to be held Saturday night at Seattle's General Petroleum Museum. Guests may wear black-tie attire or may dress in costume in accordance with this year's theme: a history of "Roadside Attractions."

The theme originated from a vote, conducted by event officials, of UW architecture students, and consists of a little-known area in architectural history.

The second floor of the General Petroleum Museum is preserved as a warehouse, complete with authentic, turn-of-the-century gas pumps, road signs, and vending areas.

"It's going to be an incredible event, one of the classiest events to hit this campus in years," gushed Nancy Cleminshaw, of the sponsoring UW Alumni Association.

Item 2:

An abused wife and her daughter will speak about domestic violence tonight at 7 p.m. in HUB 200C.

The speaker is Delia Alaniz, the Sedro Woolley woman convicted last year of hiring a gunman to kill her abusive husband. She was recently granted clemency by Governor Booth Gardner.

Part of her commuted sentence is an obligation to work volunteer hours for agencies dealing with victims of domestic violence, such as New Beginnings, and to speak on the experience.

During the one-hour presentation, Alaniz will speak "on her experience and the experience of women facing domestic violence in general," said Ann Yoder, director of the ASUW Women's Commission.

"She has a lot to say about what society is facing, how many women are being abused, and so on."

Alaniz's daughter, Dominga, will speak on "how violence against a wife affects the whole family." A question and answer period will follow.

Alaniz had been married for 17 ½ years, which she described as a period of constant abuse, including the beating and sexual abuse of Alaniz and her children. Although she had tried separation and restraining orders to keep her husband away, he kept returning to beat her up, she said.

She was imprisoned in February 1988, accused of killing her husband. In December she received a sentence of 10 years in a plea-bargaining agreement for second-degree murder. After a state-wide petition for clemency was circulated, the governor granted her clemency Sept. 8, 1989, and signed it Oct. 26. Alaniz was released from prison the following day.

The hired gunman, Michael Earls, is serving a 28-year sentence in prison. He was hired by Alaniz shortly after being released from a 10-year prison sentence for armed robbery and beating two prostitutes with a coat hanger.

In addition to five years of community service, Alaniz's revised sentence calls for counseling for herself and her children, and employment or involvement with an educational center. Also, she may not use alcohol, tobacco, or firearms and may not cohabitate with another adult without the consent of a community corrections officer.

Since the clemency petition, the state Legislature introduced and passed a bill lowering the penalties for victims of domestic violence who act against their spouses.

"There's an understanding that it is self-defense," said Beatrice Alvarez of the ASUW Women's Commission.

Item 3:

The University of Washington School of Dentistry is looking for volunteers for a federally funded study by the university and four other schools across the nation.

The purpose of the study is to evaluate the effectiveness of intravenous sedative drugs presently used by oral surgeons in the United States and other countries. Free dental care will be provided for qualifying volunteers.

To qualify, volunteers must have a minimum of two wisdom teeth, one of which must be impacted (teeth that have not yet broken through the surface of the gums). Student volunteers needs to be at least 18, in good physical condition, and free from alcohol or drug abuse.

Volunteers will be accepted through June 30. For more information, call Corla, the volunteer coordinator, at 543–2034.

14 | Writing Technical and Science News

How are science and technology covered in your local news media? Does your local newspaper or television station have a science and technology beat reporter?

If there is someone on the news staff who specializes in covering science, review some of that reporter's recent stories. How are these stories localized for readers or viewers? Are the stories clear and understandable?

Compile an overview analysis of your community's science and technology reporting. You might want to develop a chart similar to those in Assignments 1.4 and 1.5 to assist you in your analysis.

ASSIGNMENT 14.2

Find a health and medicine news story that does not explain or discuss the subject of the story in an understandable manner.

It is likely the story uses complicated terminology without definitions, for instance, or assumes that you know more about the subject than you actually do. Using examples from the story, list in specific terms how the story can be improved. What are the specific weaknesses?

What is the intended audience for this news story? How does this story fail its intended audience? What could be done to correct the problem?

ASSIGNMENT 14.3

Visit one of the science departments on your campus. Which professors are recognized regional or national experts in their research specialties? What research are they currently conducting? What organization, if any, is funding the work being done? Who is assisting them?

Write a memorandum to your instructor summarizing the story potential you have identified.

(NOTE: To avoid potential problems with your sources in the department, only one student should go to a particular department on this assignment. Your instructor may want to assign specific departments to avoid conflicts.)

ASSIGNMENT 14.4

Go to the campus library and locate several major science journals or other types of specialized science publications for a particular field (for example, animal rights, astronomy, transportation, climate/environment, medicine, or exercise).

Review the most recent editions (the past year or so) for potential news stories for your campus newspaper or television station. What new developments would interest students on your campus?

After you have identified one or more story ideas, write a story proposal for your instructor-editor:

- What news organization will you prepare the story for?
- What is the audience of this news organization?
- What is the story about? Why is it newsworthy?
- What is the specific focus of article?
- What is the local angle, if any?
- What local sources (people and otherwise) can you use for this story?

ASSIGNMENT 14.5

Below is a list of science and technical subjects that are currently in the public interest. Create at least five potential news stories and major sources relating to current issues for each subject.

Your story ideas should use sources on your campus or in your community.

1. Animal rights
2. Astronomy and space exploration
3. Biomedical ethics
4. Biotechnology and genetic engineering
5. Climate
6. Environment
7. Geology
8. Medicine and health
9. Nuclear energy

ASSIGNMENT 14.6

On the following pages is a copy of a press release that you have just received in the mail. After looking it over, you see a strong story possibility for your news organization's science segment/page.

Without writing the actual story, describe in 500 words or less how you would approach this story. What sources would you use? What would be the focus of your story? For print, what sort of visuals would you seek? For television, what video would you need?

Office of Public Affairs
P.O. Box 248105
Coral Gables, FL 33124
(305) 284-5500

Contact: Rosemary Sullivant
Date: July 24, 1990

US SCIENTISTS TO WORK WITH SOVIET AND NORWEGIAN GEOPHYSICAL FIRMS IN SIBERIAN SEA

MIAMI --- In an unusual joint venture, the USSR's only privately owned geophysical company, a Norwegian commercial seismic company, and an American oceanographic institution are working together to explore one of the most remote and least known continental shelves in the world. In August and September, a group of scientists, including at least one American, will conduct seismic surveys of the East Siberian and Laptev Sea aboard the ice-breaker MEZEN.

"The probability of finding oil is quite high," says Bruce Rosendahl, dean of the University of Miami Rosenstiel School of Marine and Atmospheric Science, one member of the joint venture. "The geology of this region may be very similar to that of Alaska's north slope. The results of this study should show just how similar or dissimilar these two regions are."

The continental shelf in the Siberian sea is the widest in the world. It is a passive margin, one where the continents broke apart. "Rarely have seismic data been collected so far north. We should be able to learn the answers to some important questions about this region: where did the continents break apart, what is its deep structure, and what was the nature of the movement. There are also enormous amounts of sediments on the shelf. We will be learning more about these sediments and where they came from," says Rosendahl, a geophysicist who is a specialist in rifted terrains and passive continental margins.

The Laboratory of Regional Dynamics of Moscow, the two-year-old Soviet geophysical firm, will provide the ship from which the seismic tests will be

- more -

Siberian Sea/page two

conducted. The Geophysical Company of Norway, the largest commercial seismic

company in the world, is furnishing the ship with most modern seismic equipment

and computer software available. The Rosenstiel School is responsible for

planning the scientific program, and one or more of the school's scientists will

be onboard the ship while data are being collected.

During the seismic tests, the ship will fire its array of twenty air guns to

create a very loud boom. As sound energy penetrates through the layers of

sediment on the ocean floor, some is reflected back from the boundaries between

the layers. These reflected sound waves will be detected by thousands of sensors

on the one-and-a-half mile hydrophone cable towed by the ship. The results of

these tests will provide scientists with a two-dimensional acoustic profile of the

sediments and the layers of rock beneath. "It is the geophysical equivalent of a

taking a CAT scan," says Rosendahl.

Members of the joint venture expect that the data will have commercial as

well as scientific significance. The Soviet and Norwegian firms will be marketing

some of the results to petroleum companies.

"This new agreement may set the tone for the way Soviets go about seismic

data collection in the future," says Rosendahl.

- 30 -

ASSIGNMENT 14.7

Part I

You are the science and technology news writer for a Miami newspaper. You receive the press release on the following pages among today's faxes.

How do you handle this story? Without writing the story, describe in 500 words or less how you would approach this story for tomorrow's newspaper. What sources would you use? What questions would you ask them? What graphics or photographs would you recommend? How much information do you need to write this story? How do you describe the work of this accomplished scientist in words that are understood by readers?

Part II

You are the science and technology news reporter for a Miami television station. You receive the press release on the following pages among today's faxes.

How do you handle this story for television? Without writing the script, describe in 500 words or less how you would approach this story for tonight's science segment. Would you make this a package? A shorter "reader" for your segment? What sources would you use? What questions would you ask them? What video would you need? How much information do you need to write this story? How do you describe the work of this accomplished scientist in words that are understood by viewers?

 UNIVERSITY OF

N E W S

Office of Public Affairs
P.O. Box 248105
Coral Gables, FL 33124
(305) 284-5500

Contact: Rosemary Sullivant
Date: July 30, 1990

MARTIN BECKER NAMED NEW DEAN OF UNIVERSITY OF MIAMI COLLEGE OF ENGINEERING

CORAL GABLES --- Martin Becker, associate dean of the School of Engineering

of Rensselaer Polytechnic Institute, has been appointed the new dean of the

University of Miami College of Engineering.

"We are delighted that Dean Becker has accepted this position," said UM

Executive Vice President and Provost Luis Glaser. "He is a fine addition to our

faculty."

A specialist in nuclear technology, Becker joined the faculty of Rensselaer

Polytechnic Institute in 1966 after spending two years with General Electric

Company. In addition to his position as a professor in the Department of Nuclear

Engineering and Engineering Physics, Becker has served as a consultant to various

- more -

Becker/page two

public and private institutions, including Control Data Corporation, Yankee Atomic Electric Company, General Electric Company, Los Alamos Scientific Laboratory, and the New York and New Mexico Public Service Commissions. He is a fellow of the American Nuclear Society and a senior member of the Institute of Electrical and Electronicf Engineers.

"I am excited by the prospect of working with the faculty of the College of Engineering and collaborating with the other schools in the University of Miami," said Becker.

Becker is the author of two books, The Principles and Applications of Variational Methods and Heat Transfer: A Modern Approach; an editor of twelve volumes of Advances in Nuclear Science & Technology; and author or co-author of more than two hundred technical articles on nuclear energy, electric power engineering, engineering education, and radiation interaction with electronics.

Becker graduated from New York University with a bachelor's degree in engineering science in 1960. He received his masters and Ph.D. from Massachusetts Institute of Technology. He is a licensed professional engineer in the State of New York.

He will begin his new position early in the fall. In addition to his appointment as dean, Becker will hold the Victor P. Clarke Chair in Engineering.

As dean of the UM College of Engineering, Becker replaces Norman Einspruch, who has served the school as dean since 1977 and who will rejoin the faculty after a year of sabbatical leave.

- 30 -

15 Writing Opinion

For next class, you are assigned to write a review for the campus media. The review will be written for the lifestyles section of your campus newspaper. You are advised to look at back issues from this semester to understand how the newspaper uses its reviews.

The subject matter is completely open. You can select whatever subject appeals to you. Recordings, film, theater, and book reviews tend to be used more than other types of reviews. The work that you review should be recent—within a month or so. Campus-related arts should also be given preference.

This assignment should run about 750 words (three pages) maximum regardless of which option you choose. This is to be written for publication. Absolutely no fiction! Remember you are also a reporter here.

ASSIGNMENT 15.2

You are assigned to write an editorial or column for the campus media. The column or editorial must be for your campus newspaper's opinion section or op-ed page or an editorial for your campus radio or television station.

Whether you write an editorial or a column is your choice. Similarly, the subject matter is completely open. You can select whatever subject appeals to you. However, it should be a subject that is timely and current.

This assignment should run about 750 words (three pages) for print or 1:15 for broadcast, maximum, regardless of which option you choose. Furthermore, you are expected to use real problems, issues, and sources. This is to be written for publication and for broadcast. Remember you are also a reporter here. No fiction.

ASSIGNMENT 15.3

Read today's newspaper for a review of current events and issues. Then select an issue that affects your campus or community and write an editorial on that issue. The editorial should not run more than 750 words for print or 1:15 for broadcast and should inform about the issue or offer a solution to a campus or community problem.

ASSIGNMENT 15.4

Select a current campus political issue and write a broadcast commentary on that subject, assuming it would be aired on the campus radio or television station. This commentary should not run longer than 1:00.

ASSIGNMENT 15.5

Develop a proposal for a new column for your campus newspaper. The column proposal should discuss the purpose of the column (humor, information, sports, advice, commentary, and so on), the type of writing you expect to use (first or third person), your most common sources, its frequency of publication, and average length. Then write a sample column that meets the specifications of your proposal. If you and your instructor like what you propose, take the proposal to the editors of your campus newspaper.

ASSIGNMENT 15.6

Find a controversial issue that is occurring on campus. There's always some issue from which to choose. Include student government, bookstore prices, campus food, dorm life, greek life, drop/add hassles, registration nightmares, and campus security on your list for consideration.

Report the story, as you would normally for a news story, but keep in mind that the information you gather, including any hard data and quotes, will be used in three different ways.

A. Write the news story.
B. Write a column.
C. Write an editorial.
D. Finally, write a brief essay pointing out the differences in writing style you used in each of the assignments.

Check with your instructor regarding the deadline for this assignment.

ASSIGNMENT 15.7

Write an editorial obituary on a famous person. This does not have to be for someone who died recently but you may find research easier on a more recent case. If you completed the prepared obituary in Assignment 12.17, you may base your editorial obituary on that information.

ASSIGNMENT 15.8

Using *Editorials on File* (a compilation of national and international editorials on current topics), read the selected editorial endorsements of candidates during the last presidential election. This book can easily be found in the reference department of most college and main municipal libraries.

Choose an editorial that best states its endorsement. Choose another that gives weak support for its preferred candidate. Make a photocopy of the two editorials to hand in with your essay that discusses your analysis of strengths and weaknesses of the two editorials.

ASSIGNMENT 15.9

Write either an advice, humor, or arts column that would appeal to the readers in your *hometown* community.

ASSIGNMENT 15.10

Using William Ruehlman's 10 recommendations on reviewing as outlined in this chapter in the textbook, write a review of one of the eating establishments on campus. Consider all dining services, including cafeterias, faculty club, campus club, food carts, and vending machines.

ASSIGNMENT 15.11

Read about a week's worth of editorials from your local community newspaper. Select an editorial that interests you, but one with which you sharply disagree. Using either the same background data provided in the editorial, or different data, write an editorial of the opposite position on the issue.

ASSIGNMENT 15.12

Using the same week's editorial pages in Assignment 15.11, compile the following data for an analysis of the editorial pages: (Some of the categories may overlap.)

How many editorials?
How many editorials on international issues?
How many editorials on national issues?
How many editorials on state issues?
How many editorials on local issues?
How many editorials on specialized subjects (environment, technology, space exploration, and so forth)?
During the seven-day period, how many of the lead editorials are on international, national, state, local, or other issues?
How many columns?
How many columns written by ethnic or racial minorities?
How many columns written by men?
How many columns written by women?
How many columns written by a member of the newspaper's editorial board?
How many columns written by prominent members of the community?
How many columns were syndicated?

Tabulate your findings, write a 500-word analysis of the findings, and bring it to class for discussion.

ASSIGNMENT 15.13

The following story appeared on Page 1 in *The Daily* of the University of Washington (Seattle), November 1, 1989. Read it, and using the data from the University of Washington, or updating it to get fresh responses from your college, write an editorial or column on the survey results.

NEWSPAPER: *The Daily* of the University of Washington, Seattle
DATE: November 1,1989
VOL.: 97, NO. 28
HEADLINE: UW responds to dismal survey results
PAGE: 1

For academic enlightenment, *The Daily* is proud to bring its readers a few questions from a survey of college seniors conducted by the Gallup Organization for the National Endowment for the Humanities.
(1) What are the first 10 amendments of the U.S. Constitution called?

    A. Articles of Confederation

    B. Bill of Rights

    C. Mayflower Compact

    D. Declaration of Independence

(2) In addition to writing plays, William Shakespeare also wrote more than 100 poems in the form of the . . .

    A. ballad

    B. sonnet

    C. ode

    D. elegy

(3) In which time period did the Civil War occur?

    A. Before 1750

    B. 1750–1800

    C. 1800–1850

    D. 1850–1900

    E. 1900–1950

The above questions are three of the 87 questions that the survey contained. The survey was administered to 700 college seniors on campuses all over the United States in the spring of 1989.
The survey was commissioned by the National Endowment for the Humanities, and its purpose was to see the breadth of knowledge in history and literature that college seniors had acquired by the end of their college careers.

The Gallup Organization conducted a similar survey in 1986 to test 17-year-olds for their knowledge of history and literature. In fact, more than one-third of the questions on the test for college seniors were just recycled questions from the 17-year-olds' test.

The results given in the executive summary from Gallup were not very encouraging.

"If the students' answers were to be graded, more than half of those tested would have failed. Using the standard "A" to "F" scale, 55 percent of the students would have received a grade of "F" and another 20 percent a "D". Just 11 percent would have received an "A" or "B" grade," the report stated.

Many of the questions that students missed were simple history questions, such as the one concerning the decade that the Civil War took place. On the other hand, some of the more difficult questions, such as who ruled England at the time of Spanish Armada, were missed as well.

The questions ranged widely to tap on the students' different areas of knowledge. One of the most ironic results of the test is that most college students thought that many of Karl Marx's writings were from the U.S. Constitution.

As a result of the rather dismal scores, Lynne V. Cheney, chairman of the National Endowment for the Humanities, has designed a proposal to rectify the situation. She has developed a plan called "50 hours: A Core Curriculum for College Students."

Cheney's plan calls for all college students to take the same 50 hours of core classes. The areas the plan encompasses are: culture and civilizations (18 hours), foreign language (12 hours), concepts of mathematics (6 hours), foundations of the natural sciences (8 hours), and the social sciences and the modern world (6 hours).

"A core of learning encourages community. Having some learning in common draws students together—and faculty members as well," Cheney says. Cheney conveys in her report that cohesion of students is important to the future of our world.

Cheney's plan also calls for universities to have their best professors teach these classes.

"Good teaching is crucial to the success of any curriculum, and it can take a multitude of forms. But teachers who inspire their students to intellectual engagement are themselves always engaged," she said.

To many UW students, this plan may sound a lot like the General Education Requirements required by the UW, and in fact, it is in many ways.

Both plans stress classes to give students a wide range of knowledge. The main difference between the UW's requirements and 50 hours is that the University gives its students more of a choice of classes to take, versus 50 hours' plan, which calls for all students to take the same courses.

How did the UW respond to the 50 hours plan, and to the survey in general?

Frederick Campbell, associate dean of Arts and Sciences, responds, "I think that the first thing to point out is that the kind of educational failure that we found in the student responses is not necessarily a problem with the University.

"The fact of the matter is that we wouldn't want to bend the University curriculum to teach basic facts that students have been, or should have been, presented with many years earlier in their schooling." Campbell contends that the UW teaches people "how to think, not basic facts."

College-level classes are more specialized than in high school and focus less on obtaining lots of trivial knowledge, but focus more on training students to be capable members of their professions.

Mark Patterson, director of the English Department, opined on the 50 hours requirement: "In principle, it's a pretty good idea, that, I think, it just makes a certain amount of sense that students would have a kind of common ground to walk on, or common knowledge.

"Common knowledge and shared knowledge is not a bad idea, but uniformity of knowledge seems to me to work against what universities are all about. The survey shows that, taken out of context, people don't know this kind of material. What is important is the context in which we do know these things."

Campbell and Patterson contend that a core program would not work well at the University because a core group would be hard to implement. Part of the charm of the UW is the individuality and freedom that it gives its students, they added.

Although the UW has the dreaded general requirements, students are able to decide which classes they would like to take to satisfy these requirements.

The implementation of 50 hours at the UW would be a hard process, as the University requirements would have to be discussed and changed. The administrators at the UW would have to decide which requirements are necessary and add those along with 50 hours to the core program. This would result in an increase in the already mammoth number of requirements.

"You don't necessarily get a better education with more requirements. What you get are students who try to fulfill requirements and don't see that there may be real educational reasons to fulfill the requirements," Patterson said.

The UW has a new plan called College Studies Program, which is similar to a core requirement in that it has selected courses for students to take that will link together and work as a group to satisfy the general education requirements. The College Studies Program can give UW students the structure that they want and the choice to be part of it or not.

Campbell said he thinks "college studies is a good program for students . . . it gives direction."

As the rest of the nation's colleges re-think their requirements, the UW administrators are confident in the education that they are imparting to their students.

In the scheme of things, what's more important: a doctor who knows when Christopher Columbus landed in the Americas or a doctor who knows the signs of heart disease?

The UW administration has tried to implement requirements so that students will know when Columbus did land, but focuses more on giving specialized knowledge to students in their respective fields, Campbell and Patterson said.

Oh, by the way, the answers for the three questions at the beginning of the story are as follows:

(1) B - Bill of Rights

(2) B - Sonnet

(3) D - The Civil War took place from 1861 to 1865.

Reprinted with the permission of *The Daily* of the University of Washington, Seattle.

ASSIGNMENT 15.14

In the story in Assignment 15.13, a number of paragraphs need attribution. Additionally, in some cases the reporter's opinion is clearly reflected. Underline those paragraphs or sentences, indicating at the beginning of the paragraph if attribution, opinion, or both are the problem.

ASSIGNMENT 15.15

Critique the following editorial from *The Hilltop,* Howard University's student newspaper. The newspaper's readership is primarily African-American students. Does the editorial do a good job of addressing this readership? Is there a message here, as well, for the non African-American community?

Also:

1. State the opinion of the editorial.

2. State any supporting evidence, examples, or data the editorial provides for basis for the opinion.

3. This editorial uses a summary approach (Chapter 15) from which to base an opinion. What are the three news elements the editorial writer used here to wrap his or her opinion? Was this done effectively?

NEWSPAPER: *The Hilltop,* Howard University, Washington, D.C.
DATE: Sept. 22, 1989
VOL.: 73, NO. 4
HEADLINE: It's a black thang . . .
PAGE: 8

It seems that being black has become even more confusing than ever. The new Miss America, Debby Turner, finds that because she had "nothing to do with" her racial identity, "being black is the least of what" she is.

Her parents "are in total agreement on this issue," according to the *Washington Post.* They state that "it's just incidental that she's black—just because we are. Couldn't help it." Sounds like she's inflicted with some sort of rare genetic disorder, doesn't it?

On the other hand, Mayor Marion Barry uses his race as an excuse for making obscene gestures at public events, as well as any other mistake he might make. He brings attention to his race, pointing out that whites are targeting him for attack because of it. But does he live up to the responsibilities that being an African-American entail?

And there's Donald Trump. He insists that if he had to start his business career over again, he would "prefer" to be black. Here's a man who has far more money and power than any African-American has even dreamt of, and this is what he says? This is deep.

Being black is not something to run away from like a plague, nor is it something to hide behind like a smokescreen, and it is definitely not just a good way to get ahead in business.

At the most fundamental level, being black in America means that you have a great responsibility to those who came before you and your community. We are the inheritors of a long history of struggle for total liberation which is far from over.

Can we afford to forget that we are descendants of Africans who were ruthlessly stolen away from their native land, robbed of their language, their culture, their religion, and subjected to the worst and most brutal kind of slavery the world has ever known? Is this a legacy to use as cover for failing to give quality leadership to the black community?

Must not we realize that we are also descendants of the great African civilizations of Egypt, Nubia, and Ethiopia, or Ghana, Mali, and Songhay, and many others, civilizations which formed the basis for all others? Is this a heritage to distance oneself as far as possible from?

In one way or another, all of us who arrive in positions of prominence or success owe a great debt to our ancestry and the masses of our people who have not been so fortunate. Can we now just consider our black identity to be nothing more than a "plus" on an employment application?

Now more than ever we need to take seriously the ancient Egyptian maxim, "Know thyself." Without this most fundamental form of human knowledge we will be forever lost as a people.

Reprinted with the permission of *The Hilltop,* Howard University, Washington, D.C.

16 News Feature Stories

You are assigned to take a walk around campus and find TEN news feature ideas that would be good stories for either the student newspaper or a campus television station newscast.

How would you approach each story? Give the idea and a one or two sentence summary of what the story would do for readers or the audience.

Come back to the lab and type up your list to submit on deadline.

For extra credit, if your instructor agrees, either outline or actually write one of these stories for next class.

ASSIGNMENT 16.2

You are assigned to write a 3–4 page (double-spaced) essay/description of your personal living environment. Sit in the room for a while. Listen. Smell. Touch. Taste (if appropriate). Look. Then write about it as if you were describing it in the most detailed fashion for someone who has not been in this place.

In the end, you will want to make the reader or listener sense he or she has been in your place by using the images you create in the mind.

Carefully consider the organizational plan of attack. What is the most effective way of writing this? A chronological plan? An inverted pyramid? A "geographic" plan? Essay?

ASSIGNMENT 16.3

Discuss whether news feature stories are important to the package of news presented each day in your local newspaper. Are these types of stories important for local radio and television newscasts? What function do these stories fill in the total presentation? How much of your local newspaper and favorite television station's news content each day is feature material? How much is spot news? Write 500 words maximum for your discussion.

ASSIGNMENT 16.4

What types of feature stories dominate your campus newspaper, magazine, and broadcast stations? What are the most common subjects? Are there types of feature stories that are routinely being overlooked? What subjects are overlooked? If so, what are they? Why do you think these oversights exist?

ASSIGNMENT 16.5

Take a spot news story from today's newspaper or television newscast and determine how it can be a starting point for a feature story. Is there a profile potential? A trend story? A how-to story? What other possibilities exist?

ASSIGNMENT 16.6

Select four recently published feature stories from a favorite newspaper or magazine. Or videotape four local news or network news feature stories from your favorite news programs.

Two stories should be considered "well done" stories, and two should be "poorly done" stories. When you have these four stories, analyze them in terms of what authors Clay Schoenfeld and Karen Diegmueller consider to be the eight basic elements of feature stories:

1. Appeal to people
2. Facts
3. Personalities
4. Angle
5. Action
6. Uniqueness and universality
7. Significance
8. Energy movement

Write a 500-word summary of how each story achieves, or fails to achieve, each of these eight points. Can you now see why the story "works"? Or why it does not do what it is designed to do?

ASSIGNMENT 16.7

Find three recent examples of human interest feature stories in your favorite newspaper or magazine. If you have access to a videotape recorder, videotape three television news human interest stories from a local station or network newscast. Try to find different subjects for each example.

Outline the organization of each story. Discuss the following points to each story:

- Where is the human element to the story? How does the writer use the human element in each story to give it personal appeal to readers or viewers?
- What are the emotional elements to the stories? What emotions are emphasized by the writer?
- What are the "story" elements in these stories? How is the story told? What type of story telling is successfully achieved by the writer?
- Finally, what is it about the story that makes it appealing? Interesting? Worth your time to read or watch?

ASSIGNMENT 16.8

In this assignment, you will learn how news organizations use feature stories and how news features fit into the total news package for the day or week.

Conduct an informal content study of all news content of your favorite newspaper, magazine, and television newscast for three consecutive issues or days. Subdivide feature stories according to types that are listed in chapter 16 of the text. Develop a chart similar to the model below and count stories by content type:

Date	Type of story	Location	Length	Source

Review only the news content. Advertising should not be a factor here. For newspapers and magazines, consider only the main news sections of the publications for your study.

After you have completed your monitoring, total your findings and answer these questions in a 750-word essay:

- What types of stories get the most frequent use?
- What types of stories get the most space (or time)?
- Does there seem to be a pattern of placement or positioning for news feature stories in particular?
- Where are the news feature stories coming from? In other words, are these stories mostly local sources? If not, are they news services or networks? Why?
- How important are news feature stories to the total news product you have reviewed for the past three days?

ASSIGNMENT 16.9

Develop one strong news feature story idea for free-lance sale. It can be a local story with regional or national potential or a highly specialized local story for local sale.

Go to the campus library and find a current copy of the *Writer's Market*, published annually in the fall by Writer's Digest Books, Cincinnati, Ohio. In this book, you will find thousands of publications for free-lance writers to market their work.

Prepare a list of at least 10 magazines that would possibly be interested in the news feature story idea that you have developed.

ASSIGNMENT 16.10

Scan recent copies of your local newspaper and, if appropriate, local magazines for appealing news feature stories. Try to be certain these feature stories have not yet been produced for television or radio. How would you adapt these stories, first appearing in a newspaper or magazine, for television? For radio?

Discuss in detail how the three best print feature stories you find can be adapted to broadcast. What about the audio element? Video element? Will different sources be needed? Will the story require a different angle for radio or television?

ASSIGNMENT 16.11

Create a list of the different *types* of news features you see used in your local news media. You can use the categories discussed in the textbook. Do your local newspapers and favorite magazines emphasize certain types of stories—or writing approaches—over others?

Do your local television news programs emphasize certain *types* of stories—and writing approaches—over others?

You might find it easier to compile information if you organize it in a chart such as the one below:

NEWSPAPER Type of story and frequency	MAGAZINE Type of story and frequency	TELEVISION Type of story and frequency

ASSIGNMENT 16.12

The following news feature story describes a trend among the more elite hotels in Chicago that cater to executive business travelers.

Why is this considered a feature story? What are its main characteristics that define it as a news feature?

What makes this story interesting to readers of the newspaper? Readers in Chicago? From other places?

How do you feel about the sources used by the writer? Are they appropriate? Adequate?

What are the strengths of this story? What are the major weaknesses? How could it be improved?

Does the subject here have potential as a "trend" story about hotels in a major city near you? How would you handle it in your nearest metropolitan area? What sources would you use? How would you contact these sources?

Write a 500-word analysis of this news feature focusing on the answers to these questions. Be sure to include any other observations you may have about the story.

SOURCE: *The Chicago Tribune*
AUTHOR: William Rice
DATE: Wednesday, June 20, 1990
SECTION/PAGE: Style, Page 3, Zone: CN.
EDITION: North Sports Final
HEADLINE: Chicago Style—Hello, front desk? Get me a dietitian

Here's the latest gambit in the ongoing can-you-top-this contest among Chicago's elite hotels: Not only will the elegant, Japanese-owned Hotel Nikko feed you American, French and Japanese fare, but it will also tell you what and how to eat.

Like several of its competitors, the Nikko has a fitness center where guests and local subscription clients can work out. Like a few, the Nikko has a massage therapist on call. Now the hotel has signed up a nutritionist-dietitian to work with fitness center clients and the hotel's staff.

Noreen Luszcz, young, enthusiastic and distinctly undictatorial, charges $45 for a 45-minute initial consultation and $25 for half-hour follow-ups. She says she finds working with people who work out a mixed blessing.

"The center is oriented to hard-driving, overachieving professionals," she says. "Many of them are perfectionists, and fitness can become an obsession. The 'Go-for-it,' all-or-nothing attitude that leads them to over-exercise can lead them to be too extreme with nutrition, too.

"It's sad when people deny themselves this or that, and it can be unhealthy. There are tradeoffs, and you should be able to work at least a little bit of almost anything you want into your diet. But nutrition is difficult to understand. It has so many gray areas and variables. Eating well isn't a quick fix. It's a long-term commitment. Results-oriented people may lose interest . . . .

"At the first session we talk basics. I assess the client's diet and begin to structure an individualized nutrition plan. Follow-ups are for review of progress and discussion of specific questions on eating, food preparation and diet-related products and plans. I don't hand out 10 days of menus. It's better for them to make those decisions themselves, but I can help them understand the pros and cons of eating certain foods and warn them about fads and frauds."

Luszcz sees her work as part of what's perceived as a growing trend: Americans taking responsibility for their ongoing good health. "What's amazing to me is not that I'm here," she says, "but that the clients are here. It shows to what extent people and their bosses are becoming open to exercise breaks during the workday."

ASSIGNMENT 16.13

Following is a short news feature "brite" that Atlanta television station WAGA-TV, Channel 5, used to end a recent newscast. It is only 26 seconds in length.

However, you are assigned to expand the story into a longer full "package" running 1:45. Read the story, then write a 250-word memo to your instructor/producer about how you would write, report, and photograph this story for the next day's noon newscast:

Wednesday, May 9, 1990

PAGE	WTR	ANC	STORY	GRAPHIC	VIDEO	TIME	OK	BKTIME
LO2	LH*	JM	POLE	POLE SITTING	VTR VO TAG	0.26	bv*	

JOHN (POLE SITTING)	FINALLY TONIGHT . . . AT GEORGIA TECH, MEMBERS OF THETA XI ("zye") FRATERNITY ARE "POLE SITTING" TO RAISE MONEY FOR MULTIPLE SCLEROSIS.
VTR/VO 00–:26	THE FRATERNITY BROTHERS HAVE BUILT A SMALL PLATFORM ON THE POLE AND ARE TAKING TURNS SITTING ON IT.
SVF:GEORGIA TECH TODAY	THEY HAVE A MOBILE PHONE TO TAKE DONATIONS FOR M-S . . . AND THAT NUMBER IS 5–8–0—7–7–3–9. THEY'LL BE POLE SITTING UNTIL NOON ON SATURDAY.
JOHN CU	ALREADY THE FRATERNITY HAS RAISED SIX HUNDRED DOLLARS AND HOPES TO COLLECT A THOUSAND BY THE END OF THE WEEK.

ASSIGNMENT 16.14

Following is a short news story that Atlanta television station WAGA-TV, Channel 5, used as an anchor "reader" in the middle of a newscast. It is only 45 seconds in length.

However, you are now assigned to update and to expand the story into a longer full "package" running 1:45. Read the story, then write a 250-word memo to your instructor/producer about how you would write, report, and photograph this story for the next day's noon newscast:

Tuesday, May 8, 1990

PAGE	WTR	ANC	STORY	GRAPHIC	VIDEO	TIME	OK	BKTIME
AO6	LW*	JA	MEASLES	MED EMERG.	VTR/VO/TAG	0.45	*	

AMANDA/MED EMERGENCY	THE UNIVERSITY OF GEORGIA REMAINS IN A STATE OF EMERGENCY TODAY . . .
	—AN OUTBREAK OF MEASLES HAS FORCED A MANDATORY VACCINATION PROGRAM AT THE SCHOOL . . .
VO/VTR :00 - :22	—RIGHT NOW, THERE IS A TWO-HOUR WAIT AT THE CAMPUS STUDENT CENTER FOR AN INOCULATION.
FONT: ATHENS, GA THIS MORNING	—THE ENTIRE UNIVERSITY STAFF, AND STUDENT BODY . . . 20-THOUSAND IN ALL . . . ARE REQUIRED TO UNDERGO THE IMMUNIZATION PROGRAM . . .
:10	—28 CASES OF MEASLES HAVE BEEN REPORTED IN ATHENS IN THE PAST TWO WEEKS . . .
	—CAMPUS DOCTORS HAD SUGGESTED SINCE LATE APRIL THAT STUDENTS BE IMMUNIZED . . . BUT TODAY MOST SAID THEY IGNORED THE WARNINGS UNTIL THE LAST MINUTE.
VTR/SOT :22–:45 FONT: DOUG TROTT AUGUSTA, GA FONT: WENDY SMITH FAYETTEVILLE, GA	****(VTR/SOT) :22–:45 OUT: . . . FRIENDS ****
	MEASLES CASES AT CLARK CENTRAL HIGH SCHOOL AND ST. JOSEPHS' CATHOLIC SCHOOL IN ATHENS PROMPTED OFFICIALS TO REQUIRE SIMILAR IMMUNIZATION PROGRAMS LAST WEEK . . .

ASSIGNMENT 16.15

Below is a news feature written by Stephen Robitaille with contributions by De Tran of the *San Jose Mercury News* in California. Read it and write a 500-word analysis of this news feature focusing on the answers to the questions below. Be sure to include any other observations you may have about the story.

1. Why is this considered a news feature story? What are its main characteristics that define it as a news feature?

2. Is the lead effective? Why or why not? How is the overall organization of the story? Can you suggest improvements?

3. What makes this story interesting to readers of the newspaper? Readers in the San Jose area? From other places?

4. How do you feel about the sources used by the writer? Are they appropriate? Adequate?

5. Does the description in the story "paint" images in your mind when you read it? How do the authors achieve this?

6. In summary, what are the strengths of this story? What are the major weaknesses? How could it be improved?

NEWSPAPER: *San Jose Mercury News*
DATE: Sunday, May 6, 1990
AUTHOR/REPORTER: Stephen Robitaille, Staff Writer
(*Mercury News* Staff Writer De Tran contributed to this report.)
EDITION: Peninsula/AM
HEADLINE: Palo Alto parade put kids in charge
PAGE: 1B

Saturday was a day for adults to wear balloons on their hats, for the mayor to smile and wave to the crowd and, most importantly, for kids to have the run of the town.

It was Palo Alto's 68th Annual May Fete Parade, a grand and goofy celebration of children that has grown from its pet parade beginnings to become the oldest and largest children's parade in Northern California.

And it was Eric Jackson Ogrey's third May Fete Parade. The Palo Alto 4-year-old worked the crowd of 10,000 like the seasoned veteran he was, hauling his tricycle to a flying stop at the corner of University and Waverly Street as he shrieked with bug-eyed delight and waved to his applauding onlookers.

"Well, I like the driving," said Eric during a pause in the parade, where he sported a railroad cap and a trike festooned with balloons, crepe paper and ribbons. "And, um, I like these," said the boy, toying with the ribbons on his handlebars.

"And my name is Eric!" he shouted, smiling over his shoulder and waving as he scooted back into the flow of the parade.

Nearly 3,000 participants representing 78 organizations marched in the parade, which kicked off an afternoon-long carnival at Addison Elementary School; the Great Ice Cream Celebration and The Great Palo Alto Mutt Show, both of which took place at Rinconada Park; and the elegant, night-long 1990 Black and White Ball in downtown Palo Alto.

The parade also celebrated the 50th anniversary of the Palo Alto Children's Library and the Stanford Area Boy Scouts, and Earth Day 1990.

"This is a big challenge," said Palo Alto mayor and parade co-grand marshal Mike Cobb with a laugh, when asked about his mental preparations for the parade ride. "To my mind, it's a chance for the community to come together. It was a tradition with me; I used to watch it when I was a kid. . . . I've come full circle here."

There were Boy Scouts, Girl Scouts, Cub Scouts, and Brownies. There were bands—the Spirit of Sunnyvale Marching Band, San Jose's Independence High School Band, Palo Alto's Gunn High School Band and Jane L. Stanford Middle School Marching Band, the Palo Alto Suzuki Strings, playing the "ABC" alphabet song on a score of violins.

There were baton twirlers. There were drummers. There were floats, ranging from a papier-mache globe to symbolize Earth Day 1990 to a stuffed animal, chicken wire and tissue paper concoction that won the Children's Hospital at Stanford/Ronald McDonald House top honors in the float competition.

There were costumes—kids dressed like knights and damsels, kids dressed like bees, kids dressed like owls, kids dressed like cats, kids dressed like pioneers riding in miniature Conestoga wagons, kids on roller skates with elephants trunks and elephant ears, and at least one kid as Godzilla.

And there were hordes of parents with video cameras, who frantically ran ahead of the wee marchers and jockeyed for position before their offspring passed by.

After the 90-minute parade, participants flocked to the Addison School carnival and Rinconada Park festivities. Kids dined on health food—hot dogs, cotton candy, tacos, soda, ice cream. Mutt lovers put their dogs through their paces and Black and White Ball organizers started putting on the glitz for the grownups' nighttime frolic.

About 2,500 people wearing everything from top hats to overalls showed up at the fourth annual ball.

The ball benefits the Palo Alto Recreation Foundation, which provides primary support for city recreation events.

"It's a feast," said Mike Klynn, of Palo Alto, as he sampled food samples from area restaurants, "and the music hasn't even started yet."

The ball was to provide plenty of recreation, with three bands blasting away at three sites, and the Palo Alto Train Station converted into a vaudeville venue, complete with circus shows and whistle-stop-style entertainment.

At the Palo Alto Holiday Inn, the ballroom was to be done over in an Art Deco motif, so partygoers could swing to Don Neely's Royal Jazz Orchestra. At an outdoor tent at the rear of the hotel, the Zasu Pitts Memorial Orchestra was to perform the hits of the 1960s. And at MacArthur Park restaurant, Pete Escobedo and his orchestra were set to perform salsa and samba.

"It's real exciting to do this—it's fun; I enjoy it," said volunteer Tina Riskie of Mountain View, as she taped silver and black streamers to a set of uprights marking the way toward the outdoor tent. "It's an exciting thing to be a part of."

Reprinted with the permission of the *San Jose Mercury News*.